Outlaws of Inglewood

Cover illustration: The illustration shows Clym of the Clough, Adam Bell and William of Cloudesley as pictured in the frontispiece of *Adam Bell, Clim of the Clough and William of Cloudesle* printed in the 1680s by "A.M. for W. Thackeray at the Angel, in Duck Lane," The 17th century illustration is somewhat anachronistic. It is reprinted here by kind permission of Thames and Hudson and The Pepys Library, Magdalene College, Cambridge.

Outlaws of Inglewood
A Cumbrian Legend

The Story of
Adam Bell, Clym of the Clough and William of Cloudesley

Roger Chambers

Illustrations by Paola Fontana

Exposure

Outlaws of Inglewood – A Cumbrian Legend

The Story of Adam Bell, Clym of the Clough and William of Cloudesley

First published in 2007 by Exposure Publishing
at the Diggory Press,
Three Rivers, Minions, Liskeard, Cornwall, PL14 5LE.

Author © Roger Chambers 2007
www.roger-chambers.co.uk

Illustrations © Paola Fontana 2006–7
www.fineillustrations.com

ISBN 978-1846855412

All rights reserved. No part of this publication may be reproduced, stored in a retrieval system, or transmitted in any form or by any means without the prior written permission of the relevant copyright holder nor be otherwise circulated in any form of binding or cover other than that in which it is published and without a similar condition including this condition being imposed on the subsequent purchaser.

Roger Chambers has asserted his rights as the author in accordance with the provisions of the Copyright, Designs and Patents Act 1988.

British Library Cataloguing in Publications Data

A catalogue record is available from the British Library.

Designed and typeset by the author

For
Rosemary Ann Chambers
1941 – 2006
My wife and best friend who helped and supported me.
With love.

The forest huge of ancient Caledon
Is but a name, nor more is Inglewood,
That swept from hill to hill, from flood to flood:
On her last thorn the mighty Moon has shone;
Yet still, though unappropriate Wild be none,
Fair parks spread wide where Adam Bell might deign
With Clym o' the Clough, were they alive again,
To kill for merry feast their venison.

William Wordsworth (1770– 1850)
Lines from his sonnet
Suggested by a View from an Eminence in Inglewood Forest

PREFACE

The legend of Adam Bell, Clym of the Clough and William of Cloudesley has been known to story tellers since at least the early years of the fifteenth century and the first, full, printed account dates from around 1565.

Its setting is Inglewood, the ancient and vanished forest between Carlisle and Penrith, as well as Carlisle city itself and London. It is an exciting story of outlawry, betrayal, murder, escape from a besieged and burning house in Carlisle, a running battle through the streets of the city, and a demonstration of skilful archery in the manner of William Tell in front of the king and queen, after which ...

Outlaws of Inglewood takes the verses of the original, 16th century ballad and develops and adapts them to novel form for modern readers and, in a postscript, links the ballad to real history. The prologue is invented but, if there is invention elsewhere, this is explained in the postscript and is intended simply to make the story more suitable for twenty-first century readers by placing the original action in a historical context.

The postscript also discusses the origin and development of the legend. As with other legends, notably the chronicles of Robin Hood, its popularity generated later accounts of the lives of Adam Bell and his friends that owe little to the original legend. In at least one case, the Robin Hood story is directly linked with the outlaws of Inglewood and a television series had Robin joining forces with the Sheriff of Nottingham to rescue the Sheriff's nephew who has been captured by Adam Bell.

The postscript questions whether there were ever historical characters called Adam Bell, Clym of the Clough and William of Cloudesley and, using the hints in the legend, makes an attempt to place them in a true historical time frame.

For those wanting to know how far *Outlaws of Inglewood* departs from the original, there is a complete transcript of the original to study.

The illustrations for the book have been drawn in a 'naïve medieval' style by Paola Fontana. It is hoped that the style complements the nature of the legend. 12th century artists had only a rudimentary understanding of perspective and endeavoured to highlight the essential elements of the subject with little regard for realism.

The legend of Adam Bell, Clym of the Clough and William of Cloudesley is not so well known as it should be, despite references in the writings of Shakespeare, Wordsworth, Ben Johnson and others. *Outlaws of Inglewood* aims to bring the story to a new generation of Cumbrians of all ages as well as to the many visitors to Lakeland.

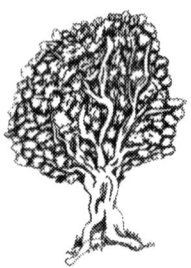

ACKNOWLEDGEMENTS

I should like to thank members of my family for their support, assistance and understanding – they helped me than they knew: Jenni; Mike and Abbie; Martin and Rosemary; and Margaret and John. Maddy, Edie and Alex helped too by distracting me when I needed distracting. I also want to thank June Freeman, John L B Bell, Stephen Bell, William Bell, Nicholas Caldwell, Wendy Hodkinson, Paul Evans, Peter Newing and Jill Blanchard who provided important help. And I also thank Paola Fontana for her patience and understanding.

PROLOGUE

> Mery it was in grene forest,
> Amonge the leues grene,
> Wher that man walke east and west,
> With bowes and arrowes kene

– I –

The watcher on Blaze Fell, had he chosen to look around, would have seen the Forest of Inglewood stretching almost unbroken from Penrith in the south nearly to the gates of the city of Carlisle in the north. Looking to the west, the forest stretched into the distance until it merged with the forests of Blencathra and Skiddaw, whilst to its east, beyond the river, it gradually blended with the king's Forest of Geltsdale and the Gilderdale Fells to their south, petering out as it reached the high ground where only scrubby birch, heather, cotton-grass and gorse managed to find a foothold on the limestone and grit moors.

Inglewood was home to a few cottagers who lived on the small plots of land they had cleared from the forest along the valley bottoms. It was a place of work to the foresters who protected the deer from the depredations of the displaced Saxon owners of the land. It was a land of quiet summer solitudes and frightening winter storms, of clear streams and black swamps, of tall trees, dense thickets and open glades. It was a land where deer, wolves, wild cat and wild boar could all be found by those with the necessary skills. And a land, too, of danger for those without such skills, or who were sought by the Chief Forester.

But William of Cloudesley had no eye for the view, indeed, like most people he knew, he felt a certain fear of the high wastes of the moors and the rocky fastnesses of the Lakeland fells – home, perhaps, to goblins or other unknown dangers. Instead, his eyes were fixed steadily on the small herd of deer which he'd been following for over an hour on that May morning and which was now grazing peacefully a few score paces away beside a hazel thicket that partly screened the view of the valley below. The nearest deer, a splendid stag with fine,

PROLOGUE

broad antlers, not yet cast, was partly hidden by some gorse bushes and William waited patiently for it to move into his vision. The slightly greater distance to the rest of the herd was no problem for a good archer, and William was as fine an archer as was to be met with in these northern forests. But he was a proud man and had an unreasoning wish to kill this magnificent beast rather than one of the smaller animals. He knew it was unreasonable – any of the herd would have provided ample meat for him and his companions – but it was still only morning and he felt that there was plenty of time to combine a skilful hunt with the search for food.

What little breeze there was came from the west bringing with it the faint, musky scent of the animals he was hunting. He knew that, although he could smell them, they couldn't smell him. The sun was behind him but, in his russet and dark green tunic, and with his back resting against the rough bark of a rowan growing just below the skyline, he felt he was unlikely to be seen. A lark, trilling as it climbed high into the blue sky, didn't disturb him. Nor, when a marten slipped with a slight rustle between some young bracken, did he move. Absolute stillness was essential if he were to remain undetected. He continued to wait. Half an hour passed and most of the herd began to move slowly down the slope. The stag moved to the right so that only its rump remained in view but William knew that its head and shoulders would emerge from the other side of the gorse if he were patient. The chest, near the shoulders, was the point to aim for if he were to kill quickly and avoid a long afternoon running down a wounded quarry. In any case, as a true countryman and hunter, he had no wish to cause the magnificent creature he must kill any unnecessary suffering. Like the deer, he too was hunted and he felt an affinity for the animal that he didn't quite recognise.

His silence, his concentration on the deer and his choice of the big stag rather than one of the other deer as his target was his undoing: without warning, a red grouse emerged from its hiding place in the bracken only a couple of paces from William's feet and, suddenly seeing the human, rocketed into the air with a clatter of wings and a frightened *go-back, go-back, back back back.* William was as startled as the bird and, when he regained his composure, it was to see the stag bounding away to join the others in their flight for the valley bottom. Even for William, such a target was not worth the risk of a lost or broken arrow. With a muttered curse, partly at the grouse and partly at his own pride in concentrating on the stag, he unstrung his bow and replaced his arrow in his belt. For a moment he thought of following the deer but, recognising the futility of this, he turned and, in a few paces, reached the summit of the fell.

Now at leisure, he stood and surveyed the main valley. Carlisle, twelve miles away to the north-west was beyond his vision but, in his mind's eye, he could make out every detail of the city. King David's grey, crenellated walls seemed to cross the horizon and, beyond, he could easily make out the whitewashed donjon of the new castle and the roof of St Mary's church where he and Alys had been married nine years before. He imagined the little house where she and the three boys lived and a feeling of despair almost overwhelmed him, knowing that they might as well have been in Scotland or France for all the good it was to him. He sighed a long sigh and, gripping his bow too tightly, he began to make his way down to the trees below.

While following the herd he had moved away from the track and the ground was uneven but he was a fit and active man and scarcely noticed the rough tussocks and brambles that barred his way. Nevertheless, he was careful to walk quietly and he constantly cast about for any sign that he was observed. When he reached the first of the forest trees, he began to relax a little and had time to wonder where his next meal might be found. Adam and Clym were for ever taunting him about his need to shoot the deer with the biggest antlers rather than any animal with meat on its bones and he was reluctant to return to their camp and explain his failure. Not that there was any need to explain himself to them, of course. Deer were plentiful in Inglewood but not so plentiful that a man who must hide from foresters was always able to find them, still less get in a shot. He didn't regard himself as a liar but would it not be true to say, "I had no chance of a decent shot all day"? At a pinch it would do as an excuse and people would believe a marksman of his reputation.

Every so often, as he walked, William paused and stood listening attentively in the peace of the forest, ears cocked for the slightest sound of deer or forester. He cautiously crossed the main road to the north and, not wishing to risk being seen by casual travellers, he took the barely visible track near the river a mile or so from Hesket. Once, when he was approaching the river, he heard the sound of men and

PROLOGUE

horses – foresters perhaps this far from the road. At all events, they were talking in the hated Norman language and, for a moment, he was tempted to try a shot at human prey but he knew it was no use and he waited quietly until the men, laughing and joking, had passed on. Nevertheless he was bitter that he had to skulk in this woodland that his forefathers had called their own while the Normans with their brutish language lorded it over Saxon serf and nobleman alike – William, dispossessed as he was, was proud that he knew none of the uncouth Norman tongue.

The sounds of the foresters faded away but the peace of the forest now seemed false. How could there be peace when the Normans claimed ownership of the trees and wild animals? Normans were allowed to hunt for sport but the Saxons weren't even allowed to hunt for food. How could that be fair? The Norman landowners, whether church or lay, were indeed jealous of their usurped rights and guarded them with vigour. Perhaps things might be a little better under the new king but many a yeoman in Inglewood, Carlisle and Penrith had fallen foul of their masters and had died on the gallows. A few lucky ones had suffered the loss of a hand or now lived solitary lives as masterless men and outlaws wherever they could find shelter.

William of Cloudesley knew he was one such lucky one – although, he felt, it seemed hard to think of luck when his Alys and the three boys were in Carlisle and he was forced to live in Inglewood. As he walked he recalled the disaster that had befallen him. It had happened last year. It was barely November but winter had come early, food had been scarce for everyone, and Alys and the boys had been hungry. The Augustinian canons at the priory had helped some people, but there were many people and little food and William and his family had gone without. The Normans, of course, had beasts in the shippen and grain in the store houses but little of it found its way into Saxon homes and most people went hungry.

William had tramped around the manors of the area but had returned, foodless and hungry, to a cold house. His neighbours, Adam Bell and Clym of the Clough were sharing a loaf with his family. When the children were asleep, the talk had turned to their problems.

PROLOGUE

– II –

"There's food a-plenty in Sowerby," said Clym.

"Deer?"

"Aye. They're coming in closer with the hard weather. Dicon was telling me he saw a good score only this morning in Cummersdale."

"Aye, and there's foresters, too," cautioned William's wife. "How many of those did Dicon see, I'd like to know? Or didn't he tell you that?"

"We might have a look," said Adam ignoring Alys.

"It's not worth it," said Alys. "You were lucky last time but there's many a good man has gone to Sowerby and Inglewood having a so-called 'look' at deer and now they have to live there all the time. And that's no good to them – nor to their wives and children neither."

"I only said 'have a look'," protested Adam.

"I know tha did, and I also ken what 'have a look' means. You've none of you to go gadding off to Sowerby – or anywhere else neither. Do you hear me, William?"

"The bairns need meat, Alys."

"They need a father more."

"There won't be bairns to need a father if we don't find them food – and soon. The little one's nought but a wisp. He won't see the winter through."

"He won't be the first to die if God wills it," said Alys. "And if God wills he won't die. If the foresters catch you at the venison, you'll lose your hands or your life and then what of me and the bairns?"

"Alys is right," said Adam. "It's not worth the risk for you. But Clym and I haven't got wife or child. We can go. You can stay here, sound in Carlisle, and look after your family. And if we're caught – well we're caught and no-one to grieve. Mayhap God'll look after us. And Dicon'll come too."

Clym nodded, "Aye. No need for you to take the risk, William."

This was not what Alys had intended.

"I'll not have any of you going," she said. She looked hard at William, "How will we feel if our friends are taken for our sakes? Tomorrow, I'll to the priory with the bairns. I'm sure the cellarer will take pity on us. I can wear that cross you gave me, William, perhaps that will help."

William laughed. "You're daft if you think a little wooden cross would stir the hearts of they heathens at the priory. They wouldn't recognise a cross if it wasn't made of gold or silver. Anyway, they helped us once and they won't help again."

"Nevertheless, I mean to try. And it's you and Clym and Adam who are daft – or worse – if you're seriously talking of going after deer. Coneys are dangerous enough but you can still lose a hand for them. Now no more stupid talk." And, with a friendly 'good night' to Adam and Clym and a kiss for her husband, she took herself off to bed.

The men exchanged glances. Adam tossed his head to one side, the ageless sign indicating 'come outside a moment and be quiet.' The others followed into the alley that ran before the house. The winter's frosts had frozen the slush and filth that was always present in the alley and, despite the cold, walking was easier than usual.

"We know what we've got to do," said Adam. "We'll wait 'til Alys gets back from the priory and then we'll be away. Fat chance of getting any alms from those Norman devils – but we can see what happens. We don't have to discuss it. We just go. All right, Clym?"

"Aye. But best leave Dicon out of it. He's not about to go running to the sheriff but fewest as knows, the better."

"But, I'm coming, too," said William. "I'm the best shot with a bow. We can take a long shot and look to see no-one comes when we've bagged a beast. Anyone who sees will come running fast enough. If we watch and anyone comes we'll have a good enough start. We ken the paths where a horse can't follow and we can beat anyone of them fat Normans on foot. If no-one comes, we can grab the deer and have it safe away and no-one any wiser."

Adam and Clym tried to dissuade William but they knew he was right. He *was* the best shot. And, especially in winter when the forest trees had no sheltering leaves and when the ground was wet under the thin ice covering, one shot would be likely all they would get.

Eventually it was agreed and the following morning when Alys dragged herself back, grim-faced, from the priory, the three men quietly left Carlisle by the southern gate and headed for Sowerby. Even to Adam and his companions, the countryside felt fresh and clean after the stench of the city's alleys.

The early frost had hardened during the night and they were able to keep close to the banks of the Caldew as it wound through the meadows towards the city. Their breath condensed in clouds as they walked and, in the frosty air, they were careful to keep their voices low to avoid attracting attention to themselves. They were unarmed as, to carry a war bow, would certainly draw unwelcome attention to them. In any case, once they reached the forest, they intended to use their shorter hunting bows which would be less cumbersome amongst the trees and branches – the three men had long ago hidden their weapons in a hollow tree at the edge of Sowerby Wood.

The friends avoided the little group of cottages at Cummersdale, turning to the right, away from the river and, with the sun at their backs, made towards Sowerby. By common consent, Adam, a tough, stocky man, well versed in the ways of the forest and the one who knew the tracks and byways best, led the way. William was next. Taller than Adam and with the long-striding, tireless gait of the countryman, he looked like everyone's idea of the true Saxon yeoman, blond, blue-eyed and clean-shaven. It was not to be wondered at that Alys had fallen for the young man who had courted her ten years before.

Clym, as always, followed the others. He was the small man of the trio, dark-haired and of slight build, he could pass by unnoticed where others would be remarked. He was the thoughtful one, the one who could fashion the straightest arrows and the one on whom everyone could rely for sound advice. They moved cautiously, slipping into the forest when they saw other travellers. People usually avoided journeys in winter but, to-day, the old Roman road was busy as people took advantage of the frost that had hardened its boggy, winter surface and made travel easier. Most were of Saxon stock but today no-one was to be trusted and it was late morning before the friends had retrieved their bows from the hideaway and were ready for the hunt.

Sowerby was merely the name of that part of Inglewood to the south-west of Carlisle that lay between the old Roman road and the river Caldew. It was flattish, gently rolling country away from the high fells with frequent open, grassy glades which, in summer, afforded pleasant solitudes and lush grass that were attractive to many a swain and his girl. They were places of sunshine and wild flowers, away from the fastnesses of the forest, where a man could feel safe from sudden attack.

But now, in winter, the glades were deserted except, if one were lucky, by the deer which could sometimes be found. The animals, hunted as they often were, preferred the denser thickets and the young leaves of the spring forest but, now, the trees were leafless and the animals were forced into the open away from the forest edge. But the forest edge was never far away and provided a measure of cover for a bold huntsman. It was to one of these glades that William, Adam and Clym directed their steps.

It was a glade they had visited before and they were pleased, but not surprised, to find a small herd of deer peacefully grazing the short, frosty turf. At this time of year there were no flies to cause the incessant flick of ears and tail that characterised the summer months and their absence provided a sense of serenity which the men were almost loth to disturb. But, 'We mun do what we mun do,' said Adam and, after waiting briefly to ensure they were unobserved, William nocked an arrow to his bow and, scarcely bothering to aim, loosed at a young stag which was about forty paces away.

The arrow flew straight to its target and, after taking barely two steps, the stag fell lifeless to the ground – a clean, satisfying kill. The rest of the herd seemed hardly aware of what had happened to their companion. They lifted their heads and looked around enquiringly and then, apparently sensing something amiss but unsure what, they cantered away.

PROLOGUE

"A good kill," whispered William.

"A bad kill," snarled Adam. "Tha should have waited for us to draw and, then, if you'd missed, we'd have had a second chance."

"But, I didn't miss," protested William. "I never miss," he added somewhat arrogantly.

"Quiet, the two of you," whispered Clym. "If any is here, we don't want them coming to see what all the blather is about!"

"Aye, shut up," said Adam.

"I didn't speak, it was .... Oh, well, never mind. Let's just be quiet." And the three of them subsided into a watchful silence.

The forest is never absolutely silent and more than once in the next ten minutes the men tensed anxiously as a small animal or bird stirred in the dead leaves of the forest floor until, at last, William deemed it safe to move.

"All right?"

"All right!"

They emerged, still cautious, from the forest and made their way to the still-warm deer.

"We mustn't tarry here. Put a cord round its feet and let's away," said Adam.

Pulling a piece of twine from his scrip, William deftly knotted it

9

round the feet of the dead animal and hefted the carcass onto his shoulders. It was best to be away from the glade as quickly as possible and the men moved away in single file towards the river, Clym and Adam going ahead as lookouts ready to call 'ware' if foresters were encountered. They followed an animal track towards the hollow tree where they intended to hide their bows and to retrieve the sacks they had hidden ready to carry away their booty.

Once at the tree, they gathered together and, drawing their knives, quickly began the unpleasant but necessary task of butchering their prey. Not that Adam, William and Clym thought it unpleasant. They didn't see the blood and gore of the deer. All they were conscious of was the joints of good, fresh meat for themselves and for Alys and the boys. They worked quickly and with concentration not noticing the little rustles in the undergrowth until it was too late.

"Stay where you are. No man to move if he doesn't want a yard of arrow in his guts." The voice was loud and rough. And menacing.

The three friends leapt to their feet, holding their knives at the ready, tightly in their hands. They were surrounded by a circle of a dozen men with bows strung and arrows nocked. Their leader, a tall man in Norman dress spoke.

"Throw knives. No move."

Even in his state of alarm, William couldn't help but notice the poor English of the Norman – and he even wondered how he could throw away the knife if he didn't move! He and his friends were easily outnumbered and their bows were hidden away, out of reach, in the hollow tree. He kept hold of his knife.

The Norman spoke again.

"Take weapons. Tie them up."

The Norman's companions, Saxon by their appearance, were all dressed in the same rough, homespun clothes and leather jerkins as Adam and his friends but with the bronze badges of king's foresters at their left breasts.

"Tie them tight. No escaping. Any escape, no reward for you. You punish as well."

Half a dozen of the foresters moved forward. They were a surly looking bunch and carried out their tasks without speaking. William couldn't tell whether they were willing servants of the Norman or whether they had been pressed into service and had no choice. They threw William and his friends to the ground and dragged their weapons from them. Resistance would have been useless – the arrows were still trained on them unwaveringly – but William managed to knee one of the foresters in the groin and got a cuff for his pains. Adam and Clym, too, made token resistance but to no avail. The more they struggled, the rougher became their assailants' actions. A big man with tousled hair and a mouth full of bad teeth hauled William to his feet again and held him tightly in a bear hug while another, younger man dragged his hands painfully behind his back and tied his hands together with a strong rope.

"He's not going to get out of yon in a hurry," he snarled. "You can let go now," he added to the older man, "it's bad enough for the poor fellow going to the gallows without having your stinking breath in his face."

The big man let go but, as he did so, shoved William away roughly so that he fell against the man who had tied his hands.

"Look what you're doing, you clumsy great lout," the man growled and then, so quietly that William scarcely heard, he muttered, "Hide this and escape if you can. Some of us will do our best for ye," and he thrust something surreptitiously into William's hand while jostling him roughly and appearing to check his knot tying.

Before William could reply, the man pushed him away and rejoined his fellows. William found himself holding the handle of a knife. The knots the man had tied weren't so very tight after all and William was able to manoeuvre the blade without being noticed into the sleeve of his tunic.

Now, armed, and with at least one sympathiser amongst their captors, he felt some hope. He couldn't speak to Adam and Clym so they knew nothing of this. They, too, had their hands tied behind their backs and, now, the young Saxon who had tied William's hands approached and tied them all three together with another length of rope which was held by one of the foresters as if they were beasts. Their feet were left untied and it was obvious they were going to have to walk. Indeed, all the party except the Norman, whose horse had been brought from where it had been tethered some distance away, were clearly going to travel on foot.

"Right! No time waste. We go now," announced the Norman and, without waiting to see if the others followed, he turned his horse and

PROLOGUE

rode off, forcing everyone else to hurry after him. He kept up a steady pace so that the foresters had almost to run to keep up and, tied as they were, it was all William, Adam and Clym could do to avoid falling – and they certainly had no breath for talking or for William to explain to Adam and Clym about the knife.

The path was wider than the one the three friends had followed earlier, for which they were thankful as the going underfoot was better with fewer ruts and hollows. After a while, the party came to a halt by the Bishop's Dyke, a raised embankment which ran through the forest and which provided a well-drained area where the ground was drier and it was more comfortable to sit.

The Norman dismounted and the foresters opened sacks which contained a rude meal of bread and meat with ale to wash it down. It was immediately obvious that only the Norman was going to have the meat and the foresters were clearly going to have to make do with just bread and ale.

It was also clear that the prisoners weren't going to have anything. Instead, the rope by which they had been led was fastened to an old tree and they were left to their own devices while everyone else ignored them.

They sat on the roots of the tree and William was able to tell the others about the knife and the man who had helped.

He spoke, his lips barely moving, "I've got a knife."

"A knife? How?"

"See yon youngish fellow over there? The one with the rip in his jerkin? With his back to us? He gave it to me. Pretended to be pushing me around and shoved it in my hand. He says some of the others are on our side and to try to get away."

"We'll never do it. The others'll be watching even if yon Norman isn't."

"It's worth a try, isn't it?" said William.

"Yes, of course. Best wait for a good chance, though."

"This may be the only chance we'll have. Can you get the knife, Clym? See if you can cut our knots without being seen."

"I'll try, but we won't have much time."

"We'll have a lot less by tomorrow. Hanging at dawn is all we can expect. They're are not going to hang about once they've convicted us."

"Is that supposed to be funny?" growled Adam.

"Funny? What do you mean?"

"You said 'hang about'. We sure will hang about. At the end of a rope."

"Oh! I see! Very funny! But we haven't time for comedy. Can you reach the knots, Clym?"

"I think so. Hey! This is my knife!"

"Never mind that. Can you reach?"

"Just move towards me a bit."

William moved a bit closer to Clym who began to saw at the ropes. His knife, as he often boasted, was as sharp as a witch's tongue and it wasn't long before William was free. With one of them free, it was quick work to cut everyone else free.

"Now," said Adam, quietly taking charge, "we wait until I say 'now' and then we're up and away. I'll go for yon big ash tree over there. William, you go right. There's a little track which is too narrow for that devil's horse and I dare say you'll give the foresters a run for their money. Clym, you head off behind us towards the beck – the trees are nearest that way. If we get away, we'll meet in that clough behind Curthwaite tomorrow. You know, where we met Dicon that time."

"Not if, when," said William.

"Eh?"

"You said 'if we get away'. It's 'when' – when we get away."

"All right. Yes. When we get away. But we go separately and split up the chase. Don't go anywhere near Carlisle. Keep in the forest. And no use trying to meet up tonight. Best leave it until we're sure we're away. We don't want one of us to lead the foresters straight to the others."

"Wait 'til they are lying down after the ale. That'll give us a start on them."

"No! They might not lie down and then we'll have lost our chance. William, you go right. Clym, you go for the beck. And I'll go straight for the ash. After that, it's everyone for himself. God speed you both."

"God speed."

"God speed."

The men waited until the foresters appeared to be laughing at some joke and then Adam said, "When I count to three, go." He paused and then, quietly, "one, two, three – GO!

The three leapt to their feet and ran. The forester who had given William the knife got in an arrow shot but he must have missed deliberately and the outlaws were away.

PROLOGUE

– III –

As he walked, William of Cloudesley recalled that awful winter's day. He and his companions had run barely a dozen paces when there was a loud shout from the Norman, and the foresters had jumped to their feet to give chase. It had been a perilous time with foresters running this way and that in pursuit and William had twice stumbled over roots and fallen branches but he'd been sure that the chase was only half-hearted and they had soon out-distanced their enemy. But the following twenty-four hours were the worst that William could remember. He had had no food and the night he'd spent in the open forest with only his jerkin to keep him warm had been awful. The worst part had been his realisation that Alys wouldn't know what had happened to him. He had only been able to hope that one of the foresters who felt sympathetic might have got a message to her.

The following day, he'd wandered tired and alone through the forest until it was safe to go to the clough at Curthwaite. It had been with immense relief that he'd met Adam and Clym and they had resolved that, thenceforth, they would swear true brotherhood to one another. This they had done in a solemn, little ceremony in front of a cross that Clym had fashioned out of a piece of oak wood. But it was days before they were able to get a message to Alys, and the messenger had brought sad news on his return – the forester who had helped them to escape had been hanged.

William and his friends had spent the next six months managing as best they could, killing the occasional deer, begging from sympathetic cottagers and, sometimes, robbing Norman travellers on the roads that ran through Inglewood. Many a baron or priest learnt to his cost that travel in Inglewood could be dangerous. But William and his friends had seldom had enough of anything. They begged and stole and hunted but they often went hungry – and some of all they managed to acquire always went to Alys and the forester's widow.

Now, with the sky blue and despite the warmth of the sun on his back, William was sad. He resolved that, whatever the dangers, he must go to Carlisle to see Alys.

The track he was following kept close to the Petteril river where the babble of the water covered the sound of his progress. Sometimes he found himself walking on the shingle margin and at other times he would climb a bluff where rocks and trees crept close to the river bed. It was at these points that he was most careful, partly because the higher elevation gave him an opportunity to look around and, partly, because, even just a little farther from the tumbling water, it was quieter and he could expect to hear walkers before they heard him. He was making his way to the camp that he and the others had established where a pile of rocks amidst a dense thicket gave them a hiding place where they could see without being seen.

Even now, in early summer, a fire was needed – to cook the venison which, he recalled all too clearly, he was supposed to have killed, but a fire, even in daylight, was always a potential hazard and at night it was too great a risk. By using dry wood, they strove to keep the smoke at bay but you could never tell and one or other of them had to keep watch all the daylight hours. Clym should be keeping a good lookout now and William resolved to test him.

He slowed his pace and took even greater care not to tread on any dry twigs. Experience had taught him how to walk quietly and to stalk the timid deer and he crept forward under the cover of some low bushes. Suddenly, he heard a low chuckle and Clym stepped forward.

"You'll have to walk quieter than that to catch me out, you noisy lout."

"I wasn't even trying," lied William but he was pleased his friend was not likely to be taken unawares by less welcome visitors.

"Where's the venison, then? Too busy stalking a sixteen-point stag to have managed even a coney? Well, well, Adam has bagged a couple of squirrels so we won't go hungry tonight – and no thanks to you." Clym led the way to their hidden camp under the little rocky crag where Adam was preparing the evening meal.

"Like you said, Adam," said Clym, "the lazy fellow hasn't shot anything."

"And, like you said, Clym, he was too busy stalking some of the king's venison. Well, what's the excuse this time?"

"No excuse," said William, "I didn't have a decent chance of a shot all day. I don't ken what's happened to the deer."

"I do," said Adam. "They've all got wise to you. They just keep their big, old stags on the far side of the herd and ken you won't take a shot at anything smaller. They're wise to you, old friend."

William protested, "No. Like I say, there was no chance of a good shot all day."

"Rubbish. A good shot like you could drop a weasel at a hundred paces. You're not telling me you couldn't get a full-grown deer at three hundred?"

William sighed to himself: his reputation worked to his disadvantage sometimes.

"I was after red on Blaze Fell," he said lamely.

"Whatever. Well, if you'll say 'sorry' you can have a share of these squirrels. But you mun make a better effort tomorrow."

"Sorry," said William. "But not tomorrow. Tonight I mean to go to Carlisle and see my Alys and the bairns."

"Say you so? Not by my advice, you won't. If you go out of these woods to Carlisle and the justices take you, your life won't be worth a groat."

"Aye, I ken that well," said William, "but, nevertheless, I mean to go. Life isn't worth much if I can never see my Alys and the three bairns again."

Clym and Adam tried all they knew to change his mind and Clym even offered to go in his place to take a message. But William was adamant, "I mean to go whatever you say. It's time for me to spend a night under my own roof."

CHAPTER ONE

> He toke hys leave of his brethren two,
> And to Carlel he is gon;
> There he knocked at hys owne windowe,
> Shortlye and anone.

The squirrels were tough – and there was very little meat for three hungry men. But, with thick bread trenchers and washed down with small ale, the meal took away the worst pangs of hunger. Adam and Clym had hoped William would have changed his mind about the dangerous trip to Carlisle but he remained determined.

"I mean to go," he said, standing up, "and I'll have to be gone now if I am to get through the city gates before curfew."

"You're not thinking of going like that," said Adam. "Alys won't recognise you with all that scruffy beard you've grown in the last months. She'll have the watch out herself if tha turns up looking like that. She'll think Old Nick himself is after her."

"It'll be a good disguise, that's for sure," laughed Clym.

"Aye. I'll be needing to keep hid from the porters on the gate. Some of them know me."

"Well, you'll have to tidy up some, or the porters'll call the watch and you'll be inside the gaol before you set eyes on Alys. Come on, if you're set on going, Clym and I'll have to shave you."

"There's not time. It's a fair step and the gates close at compline."

"There is time. You'll have to make time. It won't take long. You sit there. Where's yon knife you're always bragging about, Clym?"

William sat on the log which served the outlaws as a seat and Clym tossed his knife, handle first, to Adam who caught it deftly and made as if to attack William.

"We'll have some of that hair off as well," he said. "Might as well have him going to the hangman looking his best."

It really was the work of moments to hack off a few inches of hair and to trim the beard a little shorter and even William couldn't complain that his journey had been delayed enough to matter.

"You'd best put your sword and buckler and bow in a pack like a pedlar carries," said Adam. "It'll be a strange shape but no-one will suspect that a man on his own would hide his weapons where he can't reach them."

William had been reluctant to leave behind his bow, knowing it to be from the best timber, but he'd felt it might be too conspicuous. The compromise would have to do.

"You can stuff it with leaves to disguise the shape," added Clym.

"When you get to the gate, pull the hood down over your face. And take this staff and hobble a bit. You're wearing different clothes to those anyone has seen before."

"That merchant we had it off will recognise them, surely," said Clym. "He'd probably like them back! And the money he had in his pack."

"He was going the other way," said Adam. "Besides he'll be away to London or somewhere long since. The poor fellow will be wanting to stock up again."

"Aye. That was a good haul and no mistake. We should have kept the palfrey too."

"Not if we didn't want the merchant turning tail back to Carlisle and complaining to the justices. Best to let him get on his way to Penrith and beyond."

"He'll have sworn a complaint in Penrith."

"Well it's to Carlisle you're going so they won't be so interested. And now, you've finished with yon pack and it's you who's wasting time. God speed you and give our good wishes to Alys and the boys."

"Amen to that," said Clym.

"Thank you both," answered William, partly in gratitude for the good advice with which he'd been showered and partly in thanks for the good wishes. "I'll be away now and if I am not back by prime tomorrow, well then, you mun believe me taken or slain."

"They won't open the gates until the bell for prime," said Clym. "We'll give you an hour's good grace, it's that long from Carlisle."

William shouldered his pack and, grasping his staff and with a wave to his companions, he set off through the forest towards the track to the north.

In fact he had no serious concerns about being recognised. The months he has spent in the forest had broadened his shoulders and his face, hidden as it now was behind his beard, was more tanned with wind and sun than when he'd last passed through the city gates. With his new clothes, his hobbling gait and his hood pulled down, he felt secure. He joined the main road, relishing the sense of freedom of walking without the need to dodge into the forest at each sound. So late in the evening, there were few other travellers, for which he was glad, but when a group of pedlars hove into view he hurried to catch them up.

"Are you going to Carlisle, friends?"

"What's it to you? And who are you that call us friends?"

"A traveller like you. I would welcome the company. I have heard there are outlaws in Inglewood and it'll be dark soon."

"Aye. Well, there's five of us and only one of you so you can come along with us, if you've a mind to. But keep your distance. No offence, friend, but these are dangerous times and for all we know you could be one of they outlaws you say you're frightened of."

"Not 'frightened', just cautious. And if we fall in with any of those gentlemen, well, six staffs will be better than five."

"Mayhap. But methinks it'll be us looking after you. With a hobble like yon, you don't look as if you'd be too useful in a fight."

"I can swing a quarterstaff as well as any," answered William and whirled it round his head by way of demonstration. But it suited him to be with a group of strangers even if they were unsure of him. He had no wish for conversation but was glad of the extra camouflage that being one of a party would provide when they came to Carlisle.

He felt a lump in his throat when the city walls came into view. He had seen them, sometimes, from a distance, but seeing them now as they gradually loomed higher over their heads, brought tears unbidden to his eyes. He edged closer to his travelling companions and passed through the gates without difficulty. If the porter noticed the hobbling pedlar with the strangely-shaped pack, he gave no sign. Once through the gates, William quickly slipped away from the others and made his way through the alleys to his home. He had forgotten the dirt underfoot and the way the houses and cottages crowded together but the familiar smells and sounds brought back to him how much he'd lost.

It was dusk now and already a few of the more affluent townsfolk were lighting lamps and, passing in front of their open doors on this warm evening, he could see the cooking fires and breathe in the aromas of food being prepared. There was the sound of laughter and of babies crying. Despite the squirrels, he was hungry and even the anticipation of seeing his family didn't quite blunt the guilty thought that Alys's cooking was only a few moments away. Approaching a junction of several alleys, he jumped back in alarm as one of the town beadles came out of a doorway. This was a man who knew him well and with whom he'd even shared a stoup of ale in the past. But the man went by without recognising him and William continued on his way with even more caution.

His home was part way down a ginnel leading off one of the more important streets and he was forced to leave the shelter of the alleys temporarily and enter the busier thoroughfare. He looked about carefully, crossed to the little ginnel, and quickly made his way to his own front door. Unlike most other doorways on this warm evening, his was closed but, through the window, he could see Alys bent over the fire with her back to him. Quickly, he knocked on the window and ducked out of sight behind the shutters.

After a few moments, Alys opened the door. "Yes?"

"How are you Alys? And the children?"

Alys stared, not fully recognising him, hope and fear mingling in her mind.

"William? Is it you?"

"Aye, lass. Quickly, let in your husband – William of Cloudesley!"

Alys ran forward and threw herself into his arms. "Alas!" she sighed "It isn't safe for you. This place has been beset with people looking for you this last half year and more."

He gently disentangled himself.

"Then, since I am here and mustn't be seen, you had better let me in quickly. Fetch us meat and drink and let us be of good cheer."

He turned and shut the door behind him, bolting it as he did so. Then he went to the windows and closed and fastened the shutters tightly too.

"William. Oh, William, is it really you? I never thought to see you again in our house. Are you all right? Are you safe? Oh, William, are you all right?" And before he could assay an answer: "Where's Adam and Clym? Are they all right?"

"Aye, they are well enough. But how are you and the bairns?"

"They are fine. The little one is just beginning to walk and Will is always telling everyone what a fine man his father is and how he is going to grow up to be an archer just like you."

"He'd better not grow up into one like me. We don't want two outlaws in the family."

"Oh, William, are you sure it's safe to be here? Come, sit down there and let me get you some broth and bread. And I've got some ale. We're not rich but things are better since the summer and I can't have my husband going hungry. We've got fowls and some eggs and Dicon brought a mite of beef on Sunday. It's still all right though its been so hot. We've been eking it out. Oh, William, why ever didn't you say you were coming? I could have got something special. And you're sure you're all right? And Adam and Clym? Oh, let me look at you!" She turned again to gaze at him.

William laughed. "It's for me to look at you. Where's the bairns?"

"The baba is asleep in my chamber – or he was until we started making all the clamour. The others are away to the market place to see what's left. They'll be back in a minute. You'd best unbolt the door or they'll be battering at it and waking the bailiffs."

William did so and looked around, "And how's Nell?" he said to the old woman who was sitting by the fire scowling at him.

"None the better for seeing you here, Master William," she said tartly, "and it's no need to ask how you are. What I want to know is why you've come back?"

"To see my wife and bairns, of course," answered William. "You wouldn't grudge me that would you?"

"You shouldn't be here. You're an outlaw for venison. You've brought enough shame on this house without coming back and causing trouble."

"That's enough of that," remonstrated Alys quickly. "He's very welcome in his own home even if he is an outlaw for venison. And you're ungrateful to talk so when, out of his charity, he has provided you with a home for these seven years when no-one else would take you in. He's a fine man and time was when a good Saxon gentleman could take deer without fear of his life. Now make no more complaints and help me with a meal for all of us."

The unpleasantness was interrupted by the sudden arrival of the two boys. They burst in through the door and stopped dead when they saw their father. Then, with a squeal of excitement, they threw themselves forward and leapt into his arms almost knocking him over.

William was almost as excited as the children and hugged and kissed them, suddenly remembering that he'd forgotten to bring them the little gifts he'd fashioned during the long evenings. Fortunately, the children were too pleased to see him to notice this omission and chattered excitedly, asking him questions to which he had no chance to respond before the next question was fired at him.

"No more questions," said Alys, "Your father looks hungry. Sit down, all of you, and I'll get some food."

She bustled about while the others sat on stools around the big oak table that, apart from a simple dresser along the wall, was the only furniture in the room. She brought out bowls of the broth she'd been making. It was good and thick, almost like a stew with pieces of Dicon's beef, and with chunks of good fresh bread to mop up the bowls, it was the best meal William had had for many a long day. There was dripping too for the last of the loaf and good ale to wash it all down.

When the meal was over, William put a stool by the wall and, rested his back against the wattle. The children sat on the floor, gazing at their father with rapt attention, and, with his wife busy with some sewing by the dying embers of the cooking fire, he told them of his adventures since he'd last seen them. It was nearly dark now and with no lamp and only two candles and only the dim light from the fire, they at first failed to notice that the old woman was no longer one of the group, so engrossed were they with everything he had to say.

It was Alys who first noticed the missing member of the household.

"Where's Nell?"

"Gone to bed, I expect. Old folks need their sleep."

"I don't trust her. She's a strange one. And she doesn't like you, William."

"It'll be all right. She's just tired and she wants us to be alone together. In any case, she can't have gone far, she's scarce set foot to ground this seven years."

"I'm going to look."

Alys disappeared into the next room and was back immediately.

"She's not there. Oh, William, do you suppose she has gone to the justice?"

"Not she. She knows I've provided her with a home and she knows how you've looked after her. She'll not forget that. In any case, the gates are shut now. There's no leaving Carlisle until tomorrow."

"Well, of course, she's not leaving Carlisle," said Alys, misunderstanding. "I ken that fine. She's gone to the justice – or the sheriff! Oh, William, what are we to do?"

"Do? Nothing. She'll not betray us. Don't fret yourself."

CHAPTER TWO

> She went unto the justice hall,
> As fast as she could hye;
> "Thys nyght is come unto this town
> Wyllyam of Coudeslè."

The old woman was making her way quickly and quietly through the dark streets of the city towards the justice hall. There was no real need for secrecy but she was a little ashamed and she was half afraid of being seen and her movements being reported to Alys. No place in Carlisle was at any great distance from any other and she was soon at her destination where she hammered at the door to gain admittance.

The steward was at first reluctant to admit her and to interrupt the meal of the justice who was entertaining the sheriff to a dinner that was rather better than the one William and his family had just enjoyed. But she was a forceful individual, quite prepared to threaten the steward with unspecified disasters if he didn't let her in and she was eventually conducted into the presence of the justice.

The justice's hall was one of the grandest rooms in Carlisle. Fully twenty paces long by twelve wide and hung with tapestries, the room was smoky from a large fire that burned in the middle of the floor which, apart from an area close to the fire itself, had been strewn with fresh rushes in which half a dozen dogs squabbled for scraps. Twenty or thirty men and women sat at tables ranged along the walls, a rather larger gathering than was usual as the justice's men had been joined by those of the sheriff's household. Across the end of the hall was another table at which sat the justice and his wife, the sheriff and his wife and three or four other notables of the city.

Nell approached the top table nervously and waited to be noticed. Now that she was in the presence of the justice and the sheriff, she'd lost some of her confidence but didn't want to be turned away before she could deliver her message. It was galling to have to wait while the important people ate from a variety of dishes being brought to them by servants and drank wine from silver goblets. She knew full well she'd been seen, but the justice continued his talk with his guests and was obviously entertaining them with some story. At length, the meal was finished and the dishes cleared away and Nell thought her opportunity had come. But the justice called for music and three musicians came forward and started to play. It was not until the end of the fifth or sixth ballad that the justice called her over.

"What do you want of me, my good woman?"

Nell approached the dais.

"My lord," she said, bowing low, "William of Cloudesley is in town tonight."

"Say you so? And how do you know this?"

"I have seen him with my own eyes, my lord."

"Well? Say some more. Where did you see him and how do you know it is he?"

"My lord, I have known the villain since he was boy and I have lived in his house these past seven years. Brought shame upon us all, he has."

"So! A fine way for you to reward his charity, to tell us of this! But, no matter, *you* shall have *your* reward from me. You have not travelled here tonight for nothing. Where, then, is the villain?"

"At his house, my lord. He came secretly just as it was going dark. His wife made a meal for him," she added spitefully. "And for his children."

"I don't need his wife. Or his children. It's the man I want."

The justice was, in fact, delighted with the news Nell had brought. William and his companions in the forest had been a thorn in his side for months and the idea of at last having him in his grasp was very pleasing. But he was not the man to talk of this with an old Saxon woman and, in truth, although he was happy to use spies, in his heart he could only despise them. He waved her away and called his steward.

"See she is rewarded. That scarlet gown, perhaps, that no longer fits my lady."

The steward escorted Nell from the hall to the screens passage where she was left cooling her heels for nearly an hour before a lady's maid brought her the gown and shooed her out of the justice hall. She felt, bitterly, that she'd deserved more consideration and a greater reward but she knew better than to argue. Protesting might well have resulted in her losing even the old gown which, for all its age, was better than anything else she had. She realised, a little belatedly, that she had nowhere to return to other than the home of the man she had betrayed for so little reward and she felt apprehension about her reception. But she felt that to deny her visit to the justice and to brazen it out might be the best defence and the best way of allaying suspicion. She hurried home.

At home, Alys and William had put aside their fears about what Nell might have been doing and, when she slipped in through the door and went straight to her couch in the back room, they each breathed a little sigh of relief and relaxed.

It was late when they heard the first sounds indicating trouble. Even a distant crowd attempting silence causes a murmur of background noise made up of whispered orders, the breathing of scores of people and the hushed shuffle of cautious footsteps. William heard the sounds at the back of his mind but, at first, in the pleasure of being with Alys, he ignored them, the alertness which was an essential part of his mode of life, being temporarily extinguished. But the noises became more obtrusive and, at length, his mind could ignore it no longer.

"There's people out there, Alys."

Alys listened and then went to open the shutters and peer outside. Hastily, she closed them.

"There's folk out there, William."

"Aye, lass."

"You mun look."

William did so and saw a great crowd of people, many bearing flaming torches or weapons. Men with halberds were at the front with some archers at the rear but he also saw the justice and the sheriff with a group of foresters. The justice had wasted no time in raising the town. William's house was besieged.

"It's the foresters, love. They've come for me."

"Alas," cried Alys. "Treason! We've been betrayed!" She hurried into the back room, grabbed a stick which she held raised in her hand and cried out to Nell, "It was you who betrayed us. You evil witch! Is this how you thank us for giving you a home?"

She started to belabour the old woman.

"Nay, that'll not serve," said William.

"Well, get her out of my house." And, then, before William could move, Alys raised her stick again. "Get you out of my house. Begone and don't ever think to come back." And she dragged the old woman to the door and, quickly unlatching it, pushed her into the street before the old woman could gather herself to reply or to deny her treachery.

Alys swiftly bolted the door after her. "Now, William, my sweet husband, my famous William of Cloudesley, go into my chamber. Mayhap we'll be safe there."

William snatched up his bow, and his sword and buckler, from their concealment in his pack and, then, struggling a bit with the encumbrance, grabbed his two eldest children who were staring round-eyed at the commotion, and chased them upstairs into the strongest room where he thought his family would be safest and where, despite the noise, the baby was still sleeping. Alys, loyally, followed him, a poleaxe in her hand.

"Anyone who comes in this door while I still stand," she declared, "will die."

William had little faith in their ability to fight off the whole town raised. There would be, he knew, soldiers out there with unlimited supplies of weapons and he was sufficient of a realist to know there was nothing they could do if his enemy was determined. And determined, he felt sure they were. Those first days in the forest after he'd been taken with the stolen deer were bad, but they were nothing to the fear and worry of the next hour. All he could think of was the danger his arrival had brought upon his wife and children. Through a chink in the shutters, William could see just how dangerous was their situation.

The scene was lit by the many torches and he could see more than a hundred townspeople gathered in the alley before the house. William was sure that a great many would be his friends and would do their best to protect him and his family at least by distracting his enemies but, in the crowd, as he'd expected, he could see both foresters and soldiers and he knew they wouldn't easily be diverted from their quarry. The sheriff and justice would surely have offered a reward to any who took him. Dead or alive, it mattered not which to the justice, but the certainty of the gallows if he were taken made him all the more determined not to be taken alive and to sell his life dearly, if his life he must lose.

He peered around the small chamber where he and his wife and children stood. The candles weren't lit and it was almost completely dark, but a glimmer of light from the torches outside shone through the ill-fitting shutters. The walls were rough daub and it was barely five paces on a side. There was no furniture save for a chest, a truckle bed for him and his wife, and three cots for the children. There was no ceiling, the room being open to the rafters, and he thought of tearing a hole in the thatch and escaping that way. Perhaps he could do so but not his wife and the little ones. The only other thing in the room was a pitcher of water. There was nothing that could be used in their defence.

The chinks in the shutters were large, too large he thought for what must serve as the wall of their fort and, even from the far side of the room, he could make out the justice with his scarlet tunic and black cloak with the wolf fur trimmings in the middle of the crowd exactly in front of one of the gaps. It was a forlorn hope but the opportunity was too good to be missed. Perhaps a dead justice would make the other besiegers think twice or at least buy him some time. Fitting an arrow to the string, he drew his bow and, for once in his life, taking careful aim, loosed his shaft. It flew straight to the target, struck the justice full on the breast – and shattered into three pieces as it hit a metal fitting.

"God's curse on his heart," muttered William, "who helped you dress this day. If your cloak had been like mine, I'd have had you for sure. The devil take buckles! "

Outside, the justice laughed, "Yield thee, Cloudesley," he called. "Throw down your bow and arrows."

"God's curse on his heart that so counsels my husband," called back Alys, the light of battle in her face.

"Never mind God's curse," said William, forgetting that he'd been offering the same curse a moment ago. "If we're to get out of this we mun look to ourselves and not wait for God. Quickly, stand these beds on end. You and the children mun get down behind them. You'll be safe for the moment."

Alys snatched the baby from his cradle and the mite woke and began to cry with a vigour that belied his size. They manoeuvred the beds on end but they fell over and the defendants had to be content with placing them on their sides. They didn't provide much shelter as the bases of the children's truckles were made of thin laths and were, in any case, no more than a half-yard wide. But they would have to serve. William pushed the three children onto the floor behind the beds. The baby had stopped crying almost as soon as he'd started and he and his older brothers were now wide-eyed with terror, their normal, safe world having apparently vanished, but young Will leapt up again.

"I can fight, too," he cried.

"What with?" retorted his father.

"I've got a bow that Dicon gave me," Will said scrambling to fetch his toy bow from under the eaves at the back of the room.

Despite the desperate situation, William smiled. "I think it'd be best if you keep behind the beds with your brothers. Look after them for me. Make sure they don't stick their heads up."

The door to William's house was stout and securely fastened and, although some men dashed forward to try battering it down, William kept them at bay with carefully aimed arrows and, eventually, none was prepared to risk a shaft. Arrows from the sheriff's archers kept William on the defensive but, in any case, there was little to be done. He had a quiver-full of arrows but the sheriff's men had the armoury of the castle to draw on and William recognised it was only a matter of time before he was beaten. He thought with bitterness about the old woman whom he'd befriended and wondered at the malice that had led to her going to the justice.

If time was on the justice's side, the sheriff was nevertheless an impatient man and resented being held at bay by a single Saxon and his wife and children. He was a trained and experienced soldier who had fought in the crusades and this impertinence was not to be tolerated.

"Hey! You! You with the brand! Fire the house!"

"But, my lord, the woman and bairns."

"You heard me. I said 'fire the house'. And burn William – and his wife and his three children."

The man still seemed reluctant to carry out his orders but another, seeing his hesitation, grabbed the burning torch from his hand and ran forward and thrust the flames near the door.

"Don't be a fool. That won't do. Where's an archer? Tie a cloth to an arrow and light it from the brand. Shoot at the thatch."

An archer came forward and, taking a piece of cloth from his pouch, he tied it round an arrow and lit it from the brand, rubbing the burning oil into the cloth. Quickly, now, not wanting to damage his bow, he loosed the shaft towards the house. It settled near the apex of the roof and the thatch quickly caught alight. And then, other men, seeing the new tactic, also fired arrows into the thatch.

"Now we shall see if *your* arrows can put out the fire *our* arrows have lit," laughed the sheriff, gleefully.

The early summer weather had been fine and dry and the flames quickly took hold and spread rapidly across the roof.

"Alas," cried Alys, "I see we shall die this day." And she clung to her children and William.

"The water, Father, the water," yelled little Will, struggling with the pitcher of water that was standing in a corner of the room.

"There's not enough for this fire, my little one," said Alys looking up at the rafters where, already, fingers of flames were showing through. "We're done for."

"Not so," cried William. "I'll have you safe yet. Fetch me sheets and we'll get out yet."

Alys hurried to do his bidding and quickly snatched up blankets and sheets from the beds. William tied them together to form a rope.

"You mun get out before the roof goes. The two little ones first, then you, then Will."

I'm not going without you," Alys protested.

"You must. Think of the bairns. They'll not harm you and the little ones."

"I am staying with you, Father," said Will.

"That's my brave son," said his father, "but, no. You mun look after your mother. She needs you. And I'll fight my way out, never fear. It'll take more than a Norman sheriff to do for your father."

While he was talking, he tied the two youngest children to the sheets. Then he opened the window at the back of the house. For some unaccountable reason, there were fewer people here and none of the foresters.

"Here is my treasure," called William. "My wife and three children. But for Christ's love do them no harm. Take your vengeance on me."

He lowered the two smallest children to the ground. Some men ran forward to take them and one passed the baby to a woman who was standing nearby.

Then Alys scrambled down the rope of sheets, half falling and half climbing, and ran to gather up her baby and her son who was standing fearfully looking up at his father and the flames. Will clambered down skilfully, time spent playing in the fields and woods with other boys paying off handsomely. He ran to join his mother. A man stooped to hold him but Will bit his hand and ducked away.

"You little, devil," grunted the man, "I wasn't going to harm you. Bring your mam and we'll get away."

He turned, and with Alys and the boys following, he slipped away from the glare of the flames while the attention of the others was focused on the burning house.

Now that William had seen his family as safe as he could arrange, he felt the immediate relief that many men feel when away from wives and children, increased this time by the knowledge that they were, at least for the time being, out of harm's way. Now, he felt, he could fight man to man and have nothing but death to fear. It was he, William of Cloudesley, the best archer in the north country, against the rest on equal terms.

And then he grinned savagely. Not much equality when his arrows were running out and there were soldiers out front and, now, at the back as well. The crackle of flames in the roof forecast the eventual outcome, but, determined not to be taken, he shot methodically, making sure that each arrow told. He saw many a forester fall, wounded or killed, but at length, reaching for another shaft, he found to his dismay that he'd shot his last arrow.

It was at that moment that some of the rafters gave way and a shower of burning thatch fell upon him. He was taken by surprise and, to his further consternation, he realised the burning thatch had burned through the string of his bow. What would otherwise have been a major disaster, was mitigated by the realisation that he had no more arrows anyway.

The burning embers of the thatch caught on his clothing and he was almost in despair when he called aloud to himself, "This is a coward's death. I would rather run and fight amongst my enemies than miserably burn to death here."

So saying, he took his sword and his buckler, and ran downstairs. Casting a swift look round his now burning home, he threw open the door and dashed outside, heading for the densest part of the crowd. As he appeared, a great roar went up from the crowd and, seconds later, there was rush of air and sparks and flames flew high into the air as the main beams of the roof of the house collapsed.

Had he waited a moment longer he would have been buried beneath the fallen roof of burning thatch. Momentarily the crowd was distracted by the shower of sparks and William struck about him with his sword, fighting so desperately and so fiercely that no man could withstand his strokes.

One, big forester, grinning fiercely, confronted him with his sword raised but William ducked under his guard and thrust upwards with the point of his own sword. The man grunted and doubled up, blood gushing from a deep wound in his belly. William dragged his sword away and slashed wildly to either side, dropping a man with each stroke. Another man, approaching from the side, fell to a swift, downward blow to his head with the pommel of his weapon.

"I want him alive," screamed the justice. "Take him alive. He'll hang tomorrow. Ten marks to the man who takes him."

The battle swayed this way and that but, although William was staying on his feet he was making no progress towards safety, "wherever that might be," he thought ruefully.

"You'll never take me, Master Justice," he yelled in bravado. "Call off your men if you don't want more to bury."

The flames had now spread to the neighbouring house and a few men, led by its unfortunate owner, turned away to fetch pails of water to try and douse them. And then another house caught and the sheriff, realising the danger, ordered more soldiers to assist in controlling the flames.

"You'll have all Carlisle burnt, Master Sheriff," gasped William.

He was now fighting with his back to his own house in the alley of flames between it and the next so he didn't see three foresters climb onto the walls of his now roofless home. The men obviously had a plan. Seizing hold of the remains of the door that had once graced William's bed chamber, they heaved it from the wall aiming to fell William with its weight. It missed, but, encouraged with their idea, they began to tear the window frames from their seatings and these they also hurled at their quarry.

The first frame caught William a glancing blow on the arm. It did him no harm but he dropped his sword. Alerted now to the new danger, he looked wildly round but there was no escape. The second frame was better aimed and felled William where he stood. With a triumphant shout, the men leapt upon the fallen outlaw, dragging him away from the burning buildings. Even now, half dazed, William struggled bravely but there were too many for one, unarmed man. William was taken.

CHAPTER THREE

> There they hym bounde both hande and fote,
> And in depe dongeon hym cast;
> "Now, Cloudeslè," sayd the hye justice,
> "Thou shalt be hanged in hast."

William was held down while strips of leather were brought, and his hands and feet were tightly bound. To make his bonds the more secure, water was thrown over the knots causing them to swell and tighten so that even were he to able to get his fingers to them, he wouldn't be able to untie them. Perhaps someone recalled that he'd escaped from captivity once before and it was intended to make sure this time.

But, this time, there was no sympathetic friend to help. Two foresters pushed a pole though his bonds and heaved the pole on to their shoulders so that he could be carried away, hanging like an animal carcass or a barrel of ale. He was clearly regarded as an important captive because a dozen foresters went in front with lighted torches held aloft to light the way, and a dozen more followed behind.

Others walked on each side. Most townsfolk now turned their attention to the burning buildings but others, eager to see what became of the famous outlaw, followed the soldiers and William. They were to be disappointed. The procession made its way to the castle drawbridge and entered the castle's forecourt. Soldiers barred the way to the inquisitive crowd.

"I am not allowing the rabble into my castle," the sheriff said to the justice. "The fellow has too many friends in Carlisle to take chances. I don't want him being helped to escape again. Take him to my deepest dungeon," he ordered the foresters.

The men, found it difficult to manoeuvre their unwieldy load along the narrow passage.

"Take the pole out, you dolts. He's not going to get away now we're in the castle," snarled the sheriff.

The men dropped their load, thankfully and none too gently, on to the stone floor of the passage and stretched to relieve their aching muscles. They removed the pole and dragged William by the shoulders, his feet trailing behind him and banging on the steps as they descended to the dungeons. It was a gloomy, dank place, the dark relieved only by the flaming torches that the men carried.

"Inside with him."

"Now, Cloudesley," said the justice, "There is no need to worry about discomfort, or about the rats, or about the food – you won't be getting any. Food I mean – there's plenty of rats – because you're to be hanged in the morning."

"One vow I shall make," said the sheriff. "A pair of new gallows will be made and all the gates of Carlisle kept fast shut. No-one shall come in. I am not having Clym of the Clough or Adam Bell coming to rescue you. No, not if they come with a thousand men or more. Nor all the devils in hell. Guard him well, master turnkey. You shall answer for it with your life if the gallows are cheated tomorrow."

The justice and the sheriff turned and left. The turnkey made to follow.

"Tha'd best not cause trouble my lad," he said to William. "There's nothing to be done. You'd best say your prayers and make your peace with the good Lord."

"Can I not have a confessor to see me?" asked William. "I'd fain see a priest to shrive me if I am to die."

"It's more than my life's worth to let anyone in," answered the turnkey. Tha mun make tha peace as best as tha can." Then, more kindly, "They do say an honest prayer from a true penitent is as good as the blessing of a rascally priest – and some of the priests here are as rascally as you could hope to find. Unless, of course, you've gold."

"I've gold enough for us both," said William. "If you can get me out of this, you can come with me to the merry greenwood and have more gold than there is in this castle."

"I meant gold for the priest! Nay, I'm married with four bairns. I can't go off to the greenwood. In any case, I'd as lief live as an honest man here in Carlisle as live as an outlaw in Inglewood. Not that you look as if you've much gold anyway."

"Then, for charity's sake, just ease my pains. Turn me on my side so the knots don't press so on my hands."

The turnkey bent and tried to make William more comfortable but there was little he could do and William resigned himself to passing a sleepless and wretched night – his last in this world if the sheriff was to be believed. With a brief nod in his direction, the turnkey left, fastening the door securely behind him and leaving William in the dark. Not a hint of light entered the dungeon and no sound penetrated. But there was the sound of dripping water and, later, when they had satisfied themselves that the humans had gone, the sound of rats rustling in the damp straw.

The morning came all too soon for William, despite his discomfort. His arms and legs were numb as a result of the awkward way in which he'd been lying with his legs and arms still trussed. In fact, he had managed a little disturbed sleep – dropping off for brief moments before cramp or the sound of rats woke him. Sometimes the rats would run across his body and, once, one actually ran over his face. He hoped they might be hungry enough to chew on his bonds and so release him but he knew it was a forlorn hope and if, by some freak chance, one had done so, he would still have been imprisoned firmly in the dungeon.

If William looked with dread on the dawn, the sheriff greeted it with eager anticipation. He wouldn't have liked to have been thought a cruel or, even, an unjust man but, like others of his class, he had very clear ideas of what was right and wrong.

Poaching deer was wrong and the time-honoured punishment for poaching deer was hanging. And when the poacher had been caught, and had escaped, and had spent the last six months or more harrying travellers on the roads that crossed Inglewood – well, the possibility of pardoning William never crossed his mind. In any case, he had killed a score or more foresters that very evening. His execution was natural and normal.

The justice, too, woke early and called his esquire to the bed chamber.

"Bring me bread and ale to break my fast. I must away to the gates at once before they are opened for the day. I'll not have that fellow we caught last night cheating the hangman. I'll not have his friends coming here to rescue him. The sheriff seems to think they are capable of anything so the gates will stay fast shut today until he is on the end of the rope."

He tore off a couple of chunks of the bread that his esquire brought, stuffed them in his mouth and washed them down with a gulp or two of ale.

"Have carpenters meet me at the market place."

Without waiting for a reply, he was on his way, hurrying through the narrow streets that, although it was nearly dawn, were still almost dark. Early risers were opening their shutters and there was the smell of freshly made bread from the bakers. The justice, however, had no thoughts for these normal aspects of an early Carlisle morning although, to be sure, he was seldom up and about so early as to be used to them. The south gate was the most urgent and he arrived just as the porter had finished opening the gates and had retired to his lodging. The justice hammered at his door.

"What's to do?" came the response. "The gates are open. Go away and let a fellow get some sleep."

"Impudence! Come, let's be seeing you. Out with you now or else you'll feel the heavy end of my staff."

The porter came slowly and reluctantly to the door, grumbling and cursing and munching on a loaf of bread.

"Your pardon, my lord, I didn't know who called. What is your will? I opened the gates promptly with the first chime of the priory's bell."

"Well, you must close them again – and quickly. The gates are not to be opened today. On your life. Keep them shut fast until William of Cloudesley has been hanged."

"But, my lord, if it pleases you, there are travellers for the market. Am I not to let them in? Look, my lord, they are already arriving."

"It does *not* please me. No-one is to come in or go out until I send word to you. I mean to hang Cloudesley today and no-one shall thwart me. And I won't have his friends coming to rescue him. Do you understand? No-one is to come in the gates until I send word. You will answer for it with your life if anyone enters."

The porter started to reply but the justice didn't wait and hurried away to take the same command to the other gates of the city. He didn't relax until he was sure that all the porters had received his instructions. Then he headed for the market place where the carpenter and his assistants were waiting for him.

"I want a pair of new gallows built. Set them up there – by the pillory."

Carlisle's market place was already busy with country people who had arrived before the gates were closed and who were setting up their stalls. And there were townspeople anxious to get the first bargains and buy the freshest produce. There were farmers with baskets of vegetables and early fruit. There were farmers' wives with eggs and squawking hens. There were some with ducks and geese and others with pails of foaming milk. Pedlars and chapmen from further afield were setting out their stalls and displaying their wares of ribbons, bolts of cloth, pins, knives, charms and trinkets of all sorts. Potters were displaying their produce, bakers and piemen were trying to entice purchasers with their strident calls and travelling apothecaries and quack doctors were offering herbs and remedies of all sorts. One man was offering to pull teeth but was attracting no customers. The pleasant aromas of new bread and pies mingled with the foul smells of the city – animals, dung, open drains and unwashed humanity. Amidst the bedlam of calls and shouts the carpenter didn't seem to understand the justice.

"Where, my lord? There's no room by the pillory. It's market day."

"I know it's market day, idiot. Do you think I cannot see it's market day? Hey! You!" he called to some of his men-at-arms who had come to the market place, sent by a quick-thinking esquire. "Move some of these stalls out of the way. I want the gallows erected right there by the pillory where everyone can see them. I'll make an example of Cloudesley that everyone can understand and if it means some of these peasants have to move, well so-be-it." And he set about demolishing a baker's stall himself.

There were wails of protest from the displaced stall holders but they were quickly silenced when the men-at-arms moved in and started clearing a large space in front of the pillory. Most stall holders, fearing for the safety of their wares, hurriedly began moving their pitches away from the busy central area they had won by arriving early and, sullenly, moved out to the less-favoured pitches around the edges of the market place. Once sufficient room had been cleared, the carpenters began their work, adding the noise of sawing and hammering to the more usual din of the market place.

"What's happening?" said the small voice of a young boy. "What is the meaning of the gallows tree?"

"It's to hang a good yeoman called William of Cloudesley," he was answered.

At first the boy didn't fully take in what he'd been told. It was not the first hanging he'd seen, nor was it likely to be the last, and, in truth, his question was more for the sake of saying something than to elicit information. But then he recognised the name. William of Cloudesley was his friend and William's wife, Alys, had often sent him secretly into the forest with food for her husband. It was not difficult or dangerous for him to visit the outlaws in this way because he was a swineherd and no-one was surprised to see him wandering off into the forest with a bundle over his shoulder, driving the swine he was paid to care for. Many a householder, including Alys herself, was grateful for his services and most were prepared to provide him with a bite to eat.

The lad didn't hesitate. Town gates weren't a problem for so small a boy and he slunk away from the market square to a place which he and the other boys knew well – a place where the walls weren't properly maintained and a slender youth could creep through a gap. No-one saw him go and he quickly made his way to the forest, keeping away from the main routes and going by animal tracks and thickets until he came to the outlaws' hideout. Clym saw him coming but he knew the lad well and made no effort to hide.

"What's aslew, lad?" he called when the swineherd came near.

"Tha looks in a right pother. Come you here and tell us what's to do."

"Where's Adam?"

"I'm here, lad. What's amiss? Have you lost your swine? We'll soon help you find them, never fear."

"It's not the swine, Adam. They're safe in Carlisle. No-one's allowed out today. All the gates are shut fast. No-one's allowed in or out."

"Well you're here. You're out."

"I ken the ways," said the swineherd in a gently superior tone, "but we're wasting time. Cloudesley is taken and condemned to death. He's to be hanged this very day as soon as they've built the gallows."

"Taken? God's mercy! I warned him! He should have stayed here with us like we told him. But he always knows best does William. He should have stayed here in the protection of the forest and we would all three of us have been safe. And out of trouble. We told him. Now, what's to be done?"

The urgency of the situation distracted Adam and Clym from their usual watchfulness and, without their at first noticing it, a deer appeared at the far side of the glade in which they were talking. When he did notice, Adam reacted instinctively. He reached for his bow, fitted an arrow, aimed and shot in one continuous movement. The deer fell dead.

Adam's reaction had been automatic, food was always a priority for the outlaws and a handsome hart was an opportunity not to be missed. But then, realising he was wasting time and that William's peril was too pressing to ignore, he cast aside his bow and said to the swineherd, "What am I thinking of? That's for your dinner, child! Run and fetch my arrow, it's too good to lose and I'll likely be needing it before long. Clym and I mun go straight away to Carlisle. By God's grace, we shall ransom William even if we pay dearly for it."

CHAPTER FOUR

> And when they came to mery Caerlell,
> In a fayre mornyng tyde,
> They founde the gates shut them untyll,
> Round about on every syde.

As the swineherd had told them, the gates of Carlisle were closed tightly and a large group of travellers was milling around in front of them clamouring for entrance. The porter was peering through a grille, telling everyone who would listen that a dangerous outlaw was to be hanged at midday and that no-one was to be allowed in or out until the justice gave permission.

"I can't let you in even if I do ken who you are," he was saying to one man dressed in fine clothing. "The lord justice says no-one is to come in at the gates even if you come from the king himself."

"What do we do now, friend?" said Adam to Clym. "We'll never get in. The lad was right. The gates are shut so tight, we'll never get in."

"The lad got out."

"Aye. I know. And I ken where, as well. But it's a tight fit for a boy. You and I are grown men – and even you wouldn't get in there, little as you are!"

"We'll need some cunning then."

"What sort of cunning?"

"Cunning cunning," said Clym. "We'll say we're messengers from the king. He'll let us in then."

"Nay. That's no good. You heard what he said to yon fellow in the blue tunic. No-one is to come in, he said, even if he comes from the king himself."

"I heard. But that was only what he *said*. He knows yon fellow wasn't from the king. If he believed we were truly from the king, he wouldn't dare keep us out. We just walk up to the gates and complain that we're being delayed and we've come with important messages from the king. We say we have had to leave our horses down the road because of the press of people and we threaten him with the king's wrath if he doesn't open the gates and let us in at once."

"It might work," said Adam doubtfully.

"Have you a better idea?"

"No. Or ... yes, I have. I have a well written letter here. If we show it to the porter and say it has the king's seal it might just work. I guess the fellow is no scholar. He might believe us if we go canny."

"Well, no time like the present. Let's try."

The two men strode boldly up to the gate and, thrusting some other people out of the way with a brusque 'king's business', hammered loudly at the hatch in the gate.

"Open up! Open up for the king's business," called Adam. And he hammered again with the pommel of his dagger, continuing to do so despite the fact that, through the grille, he could see the porter approaching.

"Who is there now?" demanded the porter. "What is all the banging? You ken full well that no-one's to come in. Not even if it were the king himself!"

"Hold your tongue, knave," said Adam. "I'll allow you're a good porter but we have a letter from the king himself for the justice and we must deliver it to him in his hall before we return to the king to tell him of the welcome we've had here."

"By Him that died on the cross," said the porter, "none shall come in 'til a false thief called William of Cloudesley is hanged."

"By the holy Virgin," said Adam, "If you keep us waiting here it is *you* who will be hanged like a thief. Look, here we have the king's seal. What, fool? Are you mad? Open up I say or it will be the worse for you!"

The porter looked at the letter and, as Adam had expected, he was unable to read the words. "Welcome to my lord's seal," he said. "For that ye shall come in. Please, my lords, don't speak ill of me to the king. I'm only a simple man trying to do his duty. We see few messengers from the king here and I was only doing the justice's bidding."

He gestured to a small door that was set in the walls a few yards away. The outlaws moved towards it and the porter opened it to let them in. Others tried to follow but Clym turned on them and said, "Ho! Keep out there! What, are you all messengers from the king? Keep out I say." He followed Adam into the city while the porter re-barred and locked the gate.

"Now, my lords," said the porter, "pray allow me to escort you to the castle. I'd fain be of assistance to such important men as the king's messengers."

"Nay," said Adam, "your work is here. You're doing a fine job – and I'll tell the king so. You mun do as you're bid by the justice but you had the good sense to let the king's messengers in. You shall be rewarded."

"Thank you, masters," answered the man, bowing low. "The king has chosen wise messengers."

Clym nodded loftily.

"To your duties, then," he said and turned away.

"Good, we're in, for which I am right glad," said Adam. "You were right, Clym, he wasn't difficult to trick. But, now we're in,

Christ who harrowed Hell, knows how we're to get out again."

"If we had the keys," answered Clym, "we could get out easily enough when the time comes."

"Aye. Well?"

The two looked at each other.

"We need the keys, Adam."

"Aye. Ho! Master Porter! We need to speak with ye again. Come here in your lodgings."

"At once, masters."

The ported led the way into his room. "Make yourselves comfortable, masters. It's not so easeful as you are wont but it serves for my needs." The room was, indeed, a small affair, no more than a closet and lit only by an arrow loop but Adam had no intention of tarrying.

"Now?' said Clym.

"Now," said Adam.

Clym moved behind the porter and, before, he was aware what was happening, seized him round the chest with one arm and placed a hand over his mouth dragging his head backwards. The man struggled against Clym's grip, at first without much conviction as if he didn't fully understand what was happening and, then, increasingly violently as Adam moved in front of him and took hold of him in a vice-like grip. He put his fingers round the back of the man's neck and with his thumbs pushed slowly upwards.

It was not easy and the man kicked and struggled, kneeing Adam in the groin. But Adam had spent six months in the forest and had had many a fight. The porter had had little to do save open and close the gates once a day and he was unused to violence. He struggled furiously but to no avail. The combined strength of Clym behind and Adam in front was too much for him and his neck slowly bent backwards until with a sickening 'crack' it broke and he fell, lifeless, to the floor.

"May God have mercy upon him," said Clym, crossing himself. "The poor fellow was only doing his duty."

"Aye. Well, it was William or him. Now, we'd better get rid of him."

"What's behind yon door?" said Clym pointing to the back of the room.

Adam crossed swiftly and threw open the door and looked.

"Well, it's a guardhouse, isn't it? It's steps to a dungeon, may heaven be praised. Give me a hand with him. He'll do all right down there. No-one is going to come looking until it's too late."

The outlaws pulled the porter's body to the door and unceremoniously dragged it down the steps to the bottom.

"That'll do. Now, let's get on and find William."

"Don't forget the keys."

Adam bent down and removed the chain of keys from the porter's belt.

"See, brother, we have the keys. Now I am the porter. The worst porter they've had in merry Carlisle for a hundred years. Now, we'll bend our bows and be into the town to rescue our brother from the clutches of the sheriff."

When they arrived at the market square, it was packed with townspeople, some busy shopping from the many stalls and others gathering to watch the execution. The new gallows stood directly in front of the pillory and, beside it, on a dais, was the justice and a group of jurors. The jurors were a sorry looking bunch, clearly brought together from the taverns of the town and it was obvious that William had already been found guilty and had been sentenced to be hanged.

"Small chance of anything else," said Clym. "Yon lot wouldn't have the guts to find him 'not guilty' if the sheriff and justice demanded otherwise."

"Be fair," said Adam in an uncharacteristically mild tone. "He is guilty. So are we all if they once take us."

William was still bound tightly by his hands and feet and lay in a cart which had been brought up to the gallows. A strong rope was fastened round his neck. Curious bystanders craned to get a good look at the famous outlaw. The justice called to a lad who was standing near the gallows.

"You there! Do you want his clothes? Come and measure him for the hanging and then you can dig his grave. You shall have his clothes. He won't be needing them much longer."

"Anyone who makes my grave will lie in it himself before long," yelled William defiantly.

The lad hesitated then came forward and, without looking at

William, began to measure him for the hanging.

The justice couldn't contain his anger at William's threat and spoke in a loud voice to reassure the townspeople. He didn't intend that people should begin to believe themselves to be cursed.

"You speak proudly, fellow, but I will hang you with my own hands. Your wickedness is over. There's no comfort for you. Neither you nor your friends in Inglewood can do anything now."

William had turned his eyes away, ignoring the justice and pretending boredom, but in doing so, he caught sight of Adam and Clym standing at the corner of the market place, bows bent and ready for action, and he felt a surge of hope. He turned his eyes back to the justice.

"I see good comfort, master justice," said William, "and, with God's will, I hope to prove you wrong. But, if I could go to the gallows with my hands free, right little would I care."

Adam Bell watched carefully.

"Brother," he said quietly to Clym, "You take the justice – that's him talking to William, the man with the fur at his collar. I'll take the sheriff. We'll shoot together and take them by surprise. If we shoot separately, one of them might get away. With any luck, we'll get William away and escape in the confusion. They'll not ken what to do with the justice and the sheriff both dead. Come behind this stall. We don't want everyone noticing."

They moved behind a stall selling pies and took up position from where they could see the gallows and cart but where they weren't easily seen by the passers-by.

"Ready?"

"Aye."

"Right. On the count of three!"

Clym nodded. Despite the noise and bustle, suddenly, the market place seemed to Adam and Clym to be unnaturally quiet and it appeared that everyone was still, so intent was their concentration and so fixed was their gaze.

"One, two, three."

They loosed their arrows on the instant. They flew through the air almost side by side almost as if they were tied together. Adam and Clym watched them go and still Carlisle seemed frozen in time. The arrows arced silently upwards and then curved silently down towards their targets, the hum of their flight overwhelmed by the noise of the market place. Each arrow, still by the side of the other, struck its man. Suddenly, Carlisle began to stir once more.

The justice fell to the ground. The sheriff fell beside him. Each man had an arrow in his heart. Men shouted and began to run. Others looked about them, not understanding what had happened. Some who happened to be close to where Adam and Clym were still standing moved away in panic, not wanting to be nearby when the soldiers and foresters began to look for someone to blame. And, perhaps, not wanting to be asked to identify the archers. Adam and Clym, taking advantage of the sudden turmoil, ran quickly towards the cart where William still lay bound. It seemed that the soldiers didn't expect the assassins to be running towards the gallows. They ran in the opposite direction, past the two outlaws, their leaders shouting to everyone to 'stay where you are', an order that no-one seemed willing to hear.

Adam and Clym jumped on to the cart and then down into its interior. They drew knives and quickly cut the bonds that held William. William tried to leap to his feet but found he couldn't. Eighteen hours tied by the ankles and wrists and unable to move had left him numb and without the strength to stand. Adam hauled him unceremoniously to his feet and thrust him against the side of the cart. Clym lightly vaulted to the ground as if he'd rehearsed the move a dozen times.

"Tha's got to stand, old friend. The foresters'll be on us as soon as they've gathered their wits. Come on! Over the side," and Adam heaved William over the side of the cart and onto the ground where Clym grasped him under the arms and steadied him.

With a determined and visible effort, William struggled to regain control of his movements and, then, seeing a soldier move towards him, he rushed upon an officer of the town and wrenched his axe from his hands. By now the foresters had realised what was happening and several of them ran towards the three outlaws.

With his newly obtained weapon, a heavy two-handed axe, William struck about him, first on one side and then on the other. It was as if he'd waited too long for the opportunity, so fierce was his attack. For a moment, the three friends were separated in the mêlée but then William found himself fighting next to his comrades as they worked their way towards the edge of the market place.

"Let's live and die together! And if we get out of this and you need me beside you, that's where you will find me."

"Look out!" yelled Clym as a great brute of a man came charging towards them.

William lifted his axe and felled him with one savage stroke. There was little room for archery in the market place so closely did their assailants press about them but, when the foresters saw the big man fall, they pulled back and gave the outlaws room to use their bows. Adam thrust a bow into William's hand.

"Here, take this and these arrows. The string is best silk."

Adam, William and Clym always felt more confident with bow in hand and arrow at the ready. Arrow after arrow they loosed into the throng which beset them. Men fell on all sides. They didn't have things all their own way, but the foresters had outlaws surrounded and were hampered by fear of who might take any arrow that missed its target.

"Don't shoot, you fool," shouted their leader at one man who had drawn his bow. "You'll kill one of us for sure. Wait until they are out of arrows and then we can close in with swords. Keep your distance for the nonce."

Gradually the fight moved from the market place and into the road leading to the town gate. Some of the townspeople seemed reluctant to join the fray. Reluctant either from fear of their own skins or reluctant to give aid to the hated foresters. By now, news of the deaths of the justice and sheriff was beginning to spread. People, drawn by curiosity and the noise, were coming to the scene of the fight and the increasing throng further hampered the foresters.

"Out of the way! Get back! Get back! There's danger here. Clear the way in the king's name," the leader shouted to the crowd. And then to the foresters, "They can't get out of the city. The justice ordered the gates closed. We'll take them at the gates."

As the battle passed through the streets, the outlaws fought together, shooting their arrows steadily and with accuracy and many of their assailants were felled or killed. But the outlaws, too, were hampered by the crowd. It was one thing to kill foresters and soldiers but they had many friends among the crowd and they didn't want innocent blood on their consciences. Indeed, most of the crowd, whether known or not, were of good, Saxon stock. Most looked on sullenly but some gave surreptitious gestures of support to the outlaws and many of the women present wailed and wrung their hands and did what they could to impede the advance of the soldiers without providing an excuse for they themselves to be attacked. The air was filled with yells and shouts and in the mayhem it was difficult to know who was friend and who was foe.

"Take care," called Adam. "we're nearly at the gates."

They turned a corner and in the distance William saw the gates closed fast against the multitude.

"They're shut," shouted William. "Make for the walls."

"No! The sallyport! I have the keys," shouted back Adam.

William accepted this surprising news without comment. He trusted Adam and Clym implicitly.

"I've no arrows left," cried Adam, throwing down his bow. "It's swords now. They'll be upon us for sure."

Clym and William, too, had used their last arrows as they had come in sight of the gates and, throwing down his bow, Clym drew his sword, brandishing it with defiance. But William had no sword and had already cast away the axe he'd snatched from the soldier in the market place. Now, he feinted left and then snatched a weapon from an unwary young forester on his right.

"Wait 'til you're older, lad, before using a sword," and he thrust the lad away from him contemptuously. Then he leapt forward again while the man was off balance and grabbed his buckler. "Ha! It's hand to hand now. Come and get us!"

It had only been seconds since they had used their last arrows and, now, there was a roar from their pursuers.

"They're out of arrows. At them now!"

It was still only mid-day – the fighting had lasted scarcely time for news to reach the castle but, of a sudden, the outlaws heard the sound of horns blown to call out the garrison and, moments later, the church bells began to peal. This was not the usual, peaceful, tuneful melody but the discordant, backward peal of the alarm that William had first heard when the Scots had invaded more than twenty years before when he was a small boy.

Very soon the small group of soldiers and foresters who had been attacking would be reinforced by many more and, despite their progress towards the gate, the outlaws' situation was growing increasingly serious. All three of the outlaws had wounds and Clym, indeed, was partially blinded from an ugly cut on the forehead which was bleeding profusely. So far none of the wounds was serious but all three realised that, with the arrival of reinforcements for their attackers, they couldn't expect to hold out much longer. They continued to fight ever more desperately.

Their arms began to tire so that they could hardly raise their swords to strike their enemies. And still their attackers came on. Now the mayor arrived with a great crowd of foresters and soldiers. For the first time Adam, Clym and William began to fear for their lives. The mayor, armed with a poleaxe, and with many well-armed followers at his back, pushed through to the front of the attackers. A sword in the hands of a tired man is no match for a poleaxe in the hands of one who is fresh. Both the mayor and William knew this. William wearily lifted his buckler to ward off the mayor's attack whilst at the same time striving to get closer to the mayor so as to be able to reach him with his sword. Adam and Clym were beset by others of the new arrivals and had too much to do fending off their own assailants to be much help to William.

The mayor saw he had William at his mercy and grinned.

"Don't yield, Cloudcsley! Prepare for death! You've cheated the gallows but you won't cheat me."

The two men circled one another whilst most of the others cleared a space to watch the confrontation. One man, however, thrust forward with a lance catching William's arm and causing him to drop his sword. With a triumphant shout the mayor brought down his poleaxe and struck William's buckler a devastating blow dashing it from his grip and almost breaking his left arm. The mayor raised his weapon again, intending to kill the now defenceless outlaw. William frantically threw himself to one side and just managed to avoid the descending poleaxe and, in doing so, tripped over his dropped sword and was able to snatch it up again.

Once more armed, but without his buckler, William slashed desperately with his weapon forcing two or three of the attackers to move back. He was then able to rejoin Adam and Clym and the three found themselves in front of the city gates.

"Keep the gates fast," the mayor ordered.

"Keep the gates closed," echoed some of the bystanders, "so the traitors can't get out."

But William, Adam and Clym had reached their first goal.

As they had expected, the city gates were tightly closed and three great pieces of timber lay across them in supporting brackets preventing their being opened. But, to one side, was the small door through which Adam and Clym had entered the city scarcely an hour before. This was only big enough for one person at a time to pass but if they could once get close to it they would be able to get out using the porter's keys.

Now they thought they had the three men cornered, the mayor and the other attackers drew back away from the reach of the flailing swords of the outlaws.

"No use more deaths – unless it's theirs," said the mayor to his followers, "we've got them now."

William and Clym stood facing the attackers whilst Adam, hidden behind them was busily trying the keys in the lock.

"The justice said he'd got me," cried William. "The sheriff said he'd got me. They were both wrong. And so are you!" he added triumphantly when, at last, Adam dragged open the little door and they saw beyond the green fields of the countryside.

Adam turned to the mayor.

"Here are your keys," he cried. "I hereby give up my new job. I find a porter's life doesn't suit me. It's too dangerous! If you take my advice you'll appoint another porter. You've had two this morning already. Now you need a third." He hurled the keys at the astonished mayor. "And curses be to any man who tries to prevent a good yeoman from coming to comfort his wife." He turned and followed William and Clym outside.

"Follow them! Take them dead or alive, but take them."

A bunch of soldiers and foresters attempted to do as they were ordered but the little door was not designed to allow the passage of squads of fully-armed soldiers, indeed it was designed specifically to make this as difficult as possible.

The ill-disciplined soldiers jammed in the doorway and the one or two who did manage to get out were deliberately hindered by all those outside who had been denied admission to the city and now saw no reason why they should help the city authorities at the expense of the fugitives.

Inside the walls, the mayor was trying to get the main gates open but was himself being hindered by the townspeople.

"The justice says they have to be kept closed," said one unhelpfully.

"Well, I say 'open them'," growled the mayor.

"The justice says to await his orders," said another trying to delay matters further.

"The justice is dead, fool. Those men have killed him. Will you wait forever?"

By the time the argument was resolved and the milling crowd cleared away sufficiently to permit the gates to open, Adam, William and Clym had gained the shelter of the nearby woods and their enemies were far behind.

"We've done it! We've damn well done it!" exulted Adam. "We've got you out and we're safe. Well done everyone!"

The three of them laughed half hysterically, half in relief, and danced like small boys.

"Hey! Hang on! If we fool about here and make all this noise, the mayor will be after us again. Who's on lookout?" said Clym. "No-one! Of course, no-one! Now, enough of this foolery. William, I'm right glad to have you safe but we mun be away from here and deep in Inglewood before we're followed."

More soberly, now, and taking proper care, the three outlaws set out for their hiding place. But, with the knowledge that they had defeated and outwitted the city authorities, they couldn't help the sense of euphoria that engulfed them. The sky seemed bluer, the sun sunnier and the leaves greener than usual on a normal May day. But they weren't so euphoric as to ignore the need for special care as they approached their trysting tree.

One at a time, and in complete silence, they entered their own, private glade set within its circle of rocks and dense bushes. It was undisturbed and, pausing only to recover fresh bows and arrows from their hiding place and to tend their wounds, they threw themselves on the ground and, for the first time that day, were able to relax. Adam fingered his bow.

"So help me, God," he said to William and Clym, "with this good yew bow in my hand I could almost wish we were back in Carlisle facing yon gang of foresters again."

All three men were, by now, very hungry and thirsty. William had not had any food since the supper with his family the previous evening and the others had not eaten since they had broken their fast that morning. Now, at peace and with a blood red sun couching beyond the trees to the west, the outlaws prepared the best meal they could, simple food but ample. Venison from the deer that Adam had shot that morning was served on silver platters that had once belonged to a fat Norman lord who had carelessly strayed into Inglewood. There was good fresh bread to mop up the gravy and foaming tankards of ale to wash all down. As night fell in the forest and the black, star-filled abyss of a moonless night replaced the blue of the day time sky, the men fell to talking and recalling the events of the past day.

"I wonder what the mayor is doing now?"

"Blaming someone else that we escaped."

"Did you see his face when you unlocked the gate, Adam?"

"He looked like someone had goosed him with a blunt sword."

"Or a red hot poker."

"Well, he won't have to explain to the sheriff or the justice how we got away."

"No. Just the king."

"I expect he'll keep it quiet."

"He'll have to tell the king. They'll have to appoint a new sheriff."

Outlaws cannot sit around camp fires as do other men – the flames attract foresters and others who spell danger. Moonless nights like this were the safest. Sometimes, under a full moon, the more hardy of the king's foresters would silently brave the terrors of the night-time forest to search for poachers or, even, to hunt deer for their own pots. But moonless nights were too dark for travel without torches, and torches gave ample warning of approaching enemies. So, despite some discomfort from their injuries but in the security of the dark night, Adam, William and Clym continued to talk over their adventures in quiet voices until the call of a hunting owl reminded them it was time for sleep. With brief 'goodnights' they eased themselves into more comfortable positions and fell asleep where they were.

CHAPTER FIVE

> As they sat in Englyshe-wood,
> Under theyr trysty tre,
> Them thought they herd a woman wepe,
> But her they mought not se.

May had seemed to be a succession of bright, sunny days and today the forest was at its loveliest. The trees were still freshly green, the woodland flowers were in full bloom and the worst of the marshy patches were drying. The three outlaws were relaxing in the warm, morning sunshine. For the moment there was little to do and if William was more than a little anxious about his wife and his burnt home, the three men had breakfasted well and game was plentiful – there was time to enjoy the peace of the forest.

At first the quiet sounds went unnoticed. But, gradually, all the men became aware of them – a gentle, keening sound like the cry of a small bird.

"What is it?" wondered Clym.

"It's a bird."

"No bird makes that noise."

"A rabbit then?"

"Nor a rabbit."

"It's someone crying."

"It's probably the mayor!" joked Adam.

"More like a child."

"I'm going to have a look," said William. "It sounds like a child. Perhaps it's lost."

He rose to his feet and walked quietly in the direction from which the sounds were coming. Partly, he didn't want to alarm the child and, partly, he didn't want himself to be taken unawares if it was not some child but a source of danger.

As he approached, he could hear that the weeping was accompanied by words spoken in a monotone, repeated over and over again as if the woman, for such it turned out to be, was repeating a well-worn rhyme.

"Alas, alas, my husband's slain. Alas, alas, my husband's slain. Alas that I ever saw this day." And, then, in a different, more angry tone, "Oh, if only I could find Adam and Clym and tell them what has happened, I wouldn't be so worried." After a pause, the monotone returned with the crying, "Alas, alas, my husband's slain."

William watched and listened, spellbound. It was his Alys and, with her, his three children clinging fearfully to her skirts. He longed to rush forward and fold them in his arms but was afraid of startling them and, in his wife's present, distracted state, causing them even greater anguish. Quietly, he withdrew and, then, approached again taking care this time to ensure that the children at least would hear. He deliberately stepped on a dry twig and coughed loudly. He turned the corner and stopped.

"Alys! Alys! Thank God we have found each other! And Will! And my two little bairns." He hurried forward and tried to sweep them all at once into his embrace. "Welcome to the greenwood, Alys, and to our trysting tree. Here come Adam and Clym, safe as you can see," he added as the two men, concerned by the noise, ran up.

Alys looked as if she had been struck by the poleaxe with which, only the day before, she had been threatening to kill their attackers in her home in Carlisle.

"By sweet Saint John," said William, "I never thought I'd see you again."

Adam and Clym stood silently watching the family reunion with the cheerfully vacant smiles of those who know that they are responsible for other people's happiness.

"William," said Alys, "I am so happy you're here. I've been frantic with worry and now I thank God we're together again."

"You must thank Adam and Clym as well. It was they who rescued me. If it hadn't been for my two good brothers here, I would be hanged on the justice's gallows by now."

"There's nothing to thank us for," said Adam with a smile as they walked back to the safety of their camp, "just be glad we're all safe and sound and together again." He paused. "I know! We must have a feast to celebrate! But, Hey! Our meal is still running around in the forest. Come on," he said, leaping to his feet, "We must go hunting."

Alys looked rather unsure.

"It'll be all right," insisted Adam. "You and the boys will be safe enough here. If you hear anything, just keep the bairns quiet – but we'll not be far away and we'll hear anything before you do and we'll be back in an instant."

Alys was not reassured. She was reluctant to let her William, with whom she had only that moment been reunited, out of her sight.

"Now, Alys, my love, " said William, "don't fret yourself, we mun eat anyway – feast or no feast. And we mustn't forget the bairns. Will," he said, turning to his eldest son, "you look after your mam. I'm leaving you in charge. Take a hold of this bow and keep a good lookout".

The bow was an adult hunting bow and was a handbreadth taller than the boy but Will took hold of it, and the quiverful of arrows his father gave him, with pride and ran to stand on a fallen tree which gave him, he thought, better views of the surrounding woods.

Alys smiled indulgently. She was proud of her eldest son who took so after his father – bold and just a bit arrogant, she thought. One day he would make some girl a fine husband. She was still frightened of what the future would bring but she understood the need to avoid alarming the children and controlled her anxiety.

A hunt took very little planning. It was only necessary quickly to check the tension of the bows and to make sure they had a quiverful of arrows each.

"No!" said William. "One shaft each. One's enough for any Saxon yeoman. One each and we have three fat deer!"

"Nay," said Clym, "That's not right. If one of us wounds a beast we mun have the arrows to go after it and finish the job. No need to cause the beast to suffer."

"You may need a dozen shafts, Clym, but I need only one. I never miss my target," boasted William.

"Well now," said Adam, "and it seems only yesterday that you came back from Blaze Fell without even a squirrel for a day's hunting. We take a quiver each for the sake of the deer. A true huntsman doesn't take risks he can avoid."

William was about to pick a fight at the implication that he wasn't a true huntsman but he recalled his recent rescue by Adam and Clym and subsided.

"In any case," continued Adam, "if we do meet with any foresters we don't want to be short of weapons. And we've got Alys and the bairns to think on."

This was true, as William knew, but he was still reluctant and, somewhat gracelessly, he stooped to retrieve his quiver from the ground.

"We'll go to Gaitsgill," said Adam as the three men prepared to leave and, with cheerful waves from Adam and Clym and kisses from William, they took their leave of Alys and the children.

At first, the path to Gaitsgill ran alongside the Pow Beck and now that William had his family near to him he, too, was able to appreciate the loveliness of the day. Through the canopy of young leaves the blue sky could be seen arching cloudlessly overhead and the mid-morning sun cast dappled shadows on the forest floor. Anemones and wood sorrel still carpeted the open ground and, under the trees, the first bluebells were beginning to appear. The flowers were late this year following the hard winter and even men who were forced to regard the forest as their workshop rather than a place for pleasure weren't immune to its splendour.

"It's a grand day, sure enough," said Clym as they walked, "and I'm right glad to have Alys and the bairns with us."

"I thought I'd lost them forever," answered William. "You and Adam were right. I shouldn't have gone gadding off to Carlisle like that. I didn't think of the risk I was running for them – or for you both neither."

"Well, it's over now," said Adam, "and all's well."

Clym was more cautious. "For the moment it is, but for how long? They're not going to let us be. They'll have the foresters out and no mistake. We'll have to think about moving away – over to Yorkshire, perhaps, they might not be so keen to cross Geltsdale."

"Why wouldn't they cross Geltsdale? If we can do it so can they. It's not as if it was winter."

"There's no love lost between Carlisle and Yorkshire," responded Clym. "If we're away from Cumberland, what's it to them where we are? No-one wants to be away from their work and their land and we aren't the only folks who like venison. They'll not follow us to Yorkshire."

"They'll send messengers, though. Think on! We slew the sheriff and the justice, and their friends on the other side of the fells won't want the likes of us around either."

"Like I said, they're no friends. But you're right. Friends or not, they've got the king's peace to maintain and they won't want the king to hear they've not done what needs to be done."

"How'll the king know?" laughed Adam. "Don't forget we're the king's messengers, Clym, and we're not going to tell him owt!"

By now, William had heard how Adam and Clym had gained passage through the city gates and he laughed as loudly as Adam but Clym, cautious as always, only smiled.

"We could try Scotland," he mused, "they can't follow us there."

"Scotland? That heathen country? I don't think so. They won't have forgotten us and there'll be folk in Dumfries or at Malcolm's court who'll recognise us easy enough." It was Adam's turn to be cautious.

"It's Alys and the bairns I'm thinking on," said William after a pause. "We three can manage right enough. There's many a lord would turn a blind eye to have us for his men-at-arms. We'd get by – but not Alys and the bairns."

"I'm not working for any Norman lord." Adam looked thunderous. "I'd rather starve first."

"They'll soon claim they're not Normans now Henry's on the throne."

"Once a Norman, always a Norman."

"Anyway, it's Alys I'm worried about really," said Clym. "Someone'd look after the bairns but Alys fought alongside of you when you were taken and she won't be safe."

"You'd best not let young Will hear you say that," grinned Adam. "He reckons he's as good with the bow as his dad. He thinks he can protect his mother as well as you. A terror he is and no mistake."

"There's the priory."

Adam guffawed. "Will? An oblate? They'd never tame young Will! He'd turn the priory upside down in a week."

The conversation went on in more muted tones, now, as they approached Gaitsgill. The forest was becoming more open and the trees more mature. Unconsciously the three men began to walk more circumspectly, taking advantage of any cover provided by the trunks of the great oaks and, after a while, the talk ceased. There had been no decision and William felt that, as the cause of the trouble, it was up to him to provide a solution.

He knew a decision couldn't be deferred indefinitely but, now, the hunt was more important and with a shake of his head he turned his attention to their quest. Spring was not the easiest time to hunt in the forest as the deer tended to be more scattered than at other times, especially autumn when the harts exercised stricter controls over their harems.

But the outlaws knew Gaitsgill well and knew the places where the deer would be most likely to congregate, so it was not long before they came upon a small herd of hinds with a few young stags grazing only fifty paces away. The outlaws approached stealthily but standing fully erect so that they could draw their bows. Adam, as usual, took charge.

"Those three by the oak?" He didn't wait for a response. "William, you take the left. Clym you take the middle. I'll take the right."

Without thought he'd given William the most difficult shot, recognising unconsciously William's superior skill. William noticed the compliment but was barely gratified by something he felt was his due. Adam continued, "On my count, together. Ready?" The others nodded. "One, two, three, shoot!"

Three bows twanged. Three arrows hummed across the glade and struck three stags almost simultaneously. With the powerful bows, the long arrows, and the short distance, the stags' deaths were almost immediate and the beasts fell where they stood. Adam let out a whoop of delight that sent the hinds and young fleeing in panic. He was about to run forward when Clym laid a warning hand on his shoulder.

"Whist, man. Where's your sense? Wait a little."

Adam looked as if he were about to argue, then he shrugged and the three of them waited in the shelter of the trees until they were certain they were alone. Quickly, then, they moved forward and after withdrawing and cleaning their arrows and returning them to their quivers, they hoisted the dead animals on to their shoulders. With the legs dangling in front, they each grasped the feet of their animal and they set off through the forest in the direction of their camp. The stags were heavy but gave no trouble to the outlaws whose muscles had been honed by months of living in the forest.

"They're good, fat beasts," said William.

"They'll serve."

With less need for silence now, the men made good time and it was not long before they were striding into their camp. Alys was busy preparing some vegetables beside a fire she had kindled and the two older boys were playing quietly with some sticks – it was a game they had invented which, so far as William could see, didn't require a winner – or loser. The youngest boy was fast asleep, curled up in a mass of roots at the base of the trysting tree itself.

"Tha shouldn't have a fire without someone to keep watch, Lass. You never know who'll be attracted by the smoke," remonstrated William quietly.

"What smoke, William?" responded his wife. "I ken the forest. This is good, dry wood. There's no smoke. Did you see any when you approached?"

William had not and, with a small shrug, he turned away to hide his anxiety. For all Alys's confidence, he knew a mistake could cost them their lives and that the flicker of flames can often be seen in the darkness of the forest when smoke is hidden by leaves. But he and the others were back now and there was no point in alarming his wife further. Now, with Adam and Clym to keep watch, he was free to help Alys with the meal of which she seemed determined to take charge.

"I've nought else for thee, Lass," he said, "but tha mun have the best beast for thyself because you fought so bravely by my side when I might've been taken or killed."

Alys smiled, "It's a wife's duty to stand by her husband. I'm only glad Adam and Clym were by yesterday. Without them you might be dead. Now, pass me yon pot."

"Aye, they're good friends," said William as he did her bidding.

"Good friends, maybe. But you wouldn't be outlaws now and the bairns without a home if Adam hadn't persuaded you to go to Sowerby."

"Hush, Lass. We might all of us have been dead last winter. The bairns needed food. We had little choice."

"We did survive though. It was difficult, especially with you away in the forest but even Nell helped."

"That witch! I'll have no talk of her."

"No more will I, but you should never have gone for venison," she paused, "but it's well over now and I'm no scold. You did what you thought best and we're safe now. We mun thank God for that."

"Aye. Are we though? There's things to think on. Inglewood is no place for a woman and bairns even in summer. And winter'll be here soon enough."

"Well, that's as may be. We've a meal to prepare and seven hungry mouths to feed even if the baba prefers the breast still."

They worked quietly together, William cutting chunks of meat off the deer and spitting it on sticks which were held close to the fire and Alys slicing roots and cutting leaves which she put in a pot boiling over the fire. It was a simple meal but, with Alys to show the way, it was the best meal the outlaws had had since they had sought refuge in the forest so many months before.

There was even some good red wine that had lately belonged to a Norman merchant who had, a few weeks previously, travelled through Inglewood without an escort. Even drunk from a horn goblet, it was a fitting end to their celebratory meal.

There was little washing up to do – spoons were sucked clean and wiped with grass, the pot, with some gravel for scouring, was swilled quickly in the beck and turned over to drain – and the friends were able to relax as the evening sun sank redly towards the treetops. It was peaceful and, sated with the meal, there seemed no need to talk.

But William had been thinking. "I am going to London tomorrow."

There was a moment's silence, broken only by the crackle of the fire.

"You're going to do what?"

"I'm going to London. I'm going to London to seek the king's pardon. If we have a letter of pardon before he hears about yesterday, we'll be all right. We can go home and no-one to stop us. You two mun come with me, and Alys and the two little ones can stay in the nunnery over at Armathwaite. Will can come with us to London – I'm not so worried about him." He turned to Will. "You're my eldest son. You shall bring word to your mother of how we fare."

Adam and Clym scarcely knew what to say but Alys was in no doubt.

"You'll do no such thing," she said. "The king won't pardon you. It's the king's own venison you've taken – and his sheriff and justice – so why should he pardon you? It's hanged you'll be and no-one to rescue you in London. It's foolish talk."

"She's right, William, the king won't pardon us. We'd just be saving him the trouble of hunting us."

But Clym was not so sure.

"We can say it was Malcolm's venison. The new king may not care so much about that. I've heard he's a fair man. Not like some of his sheriffs. He may listen if we say we were starving."

"He won't listen. Not when he hears about yesterday," said Adam.

"If we go now and quickly," said William, "he may not have heard about that. It'll only be venison. And, like Clym says, I've heard he's a fair man and loves a bold approach. He may pardon us if we plead our case."

Clym said, "It's worth the attempt. We may survive the winter but the bairns won't. And I'd as lief not live an outlaw the rest of my life. Seeing the king is our only chance. They won't rest 'til they have us after yesterday. No-one can slay a sheriff and not get hunted. They'll be away to London soon enough but we've got a day or two. They'll want to tell the king they've taken us or at least done all they can. We mun go now or it'll be too late."

Clym's opinion was usually sound but the argument went on until dark and beyond. Having once expressed her opinion, Alys remained dutifully silent but she willed that Adam, on this occasion the most cautious, would win the debate. William, recognising Clym's ability in argument, said least and listened intently as the others talked. Eventually, when, for the third time, Clym said, "It's making the effort, or dying outlaws – Alys too – and sooner not later," that Adam was persuaded.

"Well, if we're going, then best we go. No good waiting. The weather looks set fair. We go tomorrow." And he rolled himself into his cloak and settled for the night.

Before Alys could speak, William said, "You'll go to Armathwaite. The nuns'll care for you and the little ones 'til we get back."

"And what if you don't?"

"Then you'll be no worse off than you are now. There's many a widow woman in Carlisle and the nuns won't turn you out while you've got the bairns. Now, no more talk. You mun do what I say. Even Clym says it's for the best." And William turned away before Alys could reply.

CHAPTER SIX

> Thus be these yemen to London gone,
> As fast as they might hye,
> Tyll they came to the kynges pallace,
> Where they woulde nedes be.

The camp was astir before the sun had lifted itself above the nearby fells. Alys was disposed to reopen the argument but William, anticipating her, raised an admonitory hand and, with a short, "It's settled, Alys," silenced her. Breakfast was swift and with only a brief, backward glance at their camp, they made their way through the forest eastwards towards Armathwaite.

They walked in single file, Adam with Clym in front this time followed by Alys, carrying the baby, then the two older boys and William bringing up the rear. He reasoned that, although Alys might be recognised and arrested near Carlisle, this possibility was much less likely the further from the city they travelled.

The nunnery of Jesus Christ and the Blessed Virgin at Armathwaite was a Benedictine house with a reputation for charity. Isolated as it was from towns, it was unlikely that the nuns would be watching for the fugitives or that they would hand them over if they sought sanctuary – even though the outlaws had, occasionally, hunted across the nunnery's lands at Tarnwadelyn in Inglewood and, once, had taken one of the nunnery's swine which had wandered away from the herd when it was out foraging in the forest.

The journey to Armathwaite from their camp some way north of Gaitsgill was a long one for the children and it was early evening before they came in sight of the convent buildings on the banks of the little river Croglin where it joined the larger Eden.

It was felt to be safest if Alys and the children approached without an escort. A woman travelling with menfolk might be refused sanctuary and the men were wise enough to realise that their rough appearance might be interpreted as a threat. It was not unknown for desperate and masterless men to prey upon the defenceless and holy women who had dedicated their lives to the service of God.

"You mun go to the gate and ask for sanctuary for the little ones," said William. "We'll wait nearby so we can see they let you in. We'll stay until dark and then we'll be away. Don't forget to ask for sanctuary in the name of Christ and the Blessed Virgin. They won't refuse you if you ask in the name of their own patrons."

Alys was still apprehensive about the men's plan and was reluctant to be parted from William so soon after their reunion but she recognised his determination. She bowed her head obediently and, with a swift embrace for Will and a "look after your father", she made her way to the nunnery gate.

At the edge of the woodland, William, Adam and Clym watched with anxiety in case Alys was turned away. Will, however, had no doubt and it seemed he was right. Alys could be seen letting the baby pull at the bell rope and, after a moment, the gate opened. There was a brief pause... and Alys passed inside and the gate closed.

"Pray God I've done the right thing," said William, crossing himself.

The four of them withdrew a little way into the wood and settled themselves to wait for nightfall.

"We may as well camp here," said Adam, "We can't travel at night and we'll watch the gate in the morning just in case she's turned out. Not that that'll happen," he added quickly as he saw Will's sudden frown. "It'll all be well now."

But none of the adults was completely sure and they spent a restless night. In the morning they waited in sight of the gates.

Clym said, "We'll wait a wee while. Mayhap they'll decide at chapter. If she hasn't come out by mid-day, we'll ken everything is fine and we'll be away."

Adam was reluctant to wait so long. Having been the most reluctant to agree to the journey in the first place, he was now the one most keen to get away, but he recognised William's worry and settled to watch with the others. There was a moment of concern when the gate opened and a woman and child emerged but it was not Alys and they relaxed again. Gradually the sun climbed towards the zenith and they watched it begin to sink. At first William was reluctant to admit that noon had passed but, eventually, as the shadows moved round, even he was reassured and agreed to their moving off.

Travelling was never easy. The roads were poor, bridges were infrequent, and, even in summer, rain could quickly turn their surfaces into impassable mud forcing long detours. Even for a well-mounted man, the journey to London could take ten days or more and, for those on foot, the journey could be expected to last up to three weeks. For Adam, William and Clym and little Will, who, at least at the beginning, were compelled to avoid towns and villages, the journey was likely to take even longer. Will, though a sturdy lad, accustomed to travel on foot, was only seven years' old and inevitably slowed their progress but William had been determined that he would accompany them.

The first night was spent near Penrith and the second, after their first full day on the road and a cold tramp over the bleak Shap Fells, huddled in a sheep fold on the hills under Crookdale Crag. Had they but known, the deep and sheltered valley of Borrowdale was barely half a league farther on but the fold provided shelter enough for those accustomed to sleeping in the woods and they passed a peaceful night.

From then on, the adults lost track of where they were from day to day. None of them had travelled so far before and the roads they journeyed over, and the places they visited, were unknown. Whenever they met other travellers, they would ask their way to London and they became used to the slightly mystified reactions they caused. But they travelled as speedily as possible, sometimes robbing gardens, sometimes begging charity and, sometimes, as they moved further from Inglewood and the weather was bad, seeking shelter in the stables of a monastery.

They had their bows and could hunt but that slowed their progress and was to be avoided as far as possible. The weather grew hotter as the days lengthened towards mid-summer but they couldn't afford to linger if they were to reach London before messengers from Carlisle. They were well aware that such messengers were likely to be mounted and were ever fearful they would be overtaken and that news of their escape would reach London and the king before they did.

At last, twenty-three days after they left Armathwaite, they were told by another traveller that, 'yes, those are the gates of London'. They had made better time than they had dared hope but it was too late to enter the city that night – there was still nearly a league to walk to the gates and they would have closed before they reached them – so they camped again in the shelter of some trees and made a scanty supper of the dry bread they had been given the previous night.

"It's been a long walk," said Clym. "I'm not sure I'd have come if I'd known how far it was. A quick death at the end of a rope might have been easier!"

Adam grunted, "We may still have a quick death at the end of a rope. You might have the walk *and* the rope, my friend."

William, however, was more optimistic and had more regard for Will's feelings, "Stop grousing, you two. We've not come all this way for nowt. The king'll pardon us. You'll see. I feel it in my bones. Then we'll walk back to Carlisle free men."

Adam was not encouraged, "Walk back to Carlisle? I think I'd prefer the rope! You get your pardon and I'll beg for mercy – the mercy of the rope! Better a long drop than a long walk – much easier," he grinned.

"Does he mean it, Da?" queried Will with an anxious expression.

"No! Ignore me, lad. It's just my way. Although I must say I'd like a rest before we start back. No, we'll get a pardon, never fear and then we'll be four free men again."

"Four?"

"Aye, lad. Only a man could walk from Carlisle to London. And you've proved you're man enough for me." Adam gave Will a cuff which sent him reeling but left him with a grin as big as his face.

Before dawn they were at the city gates awaiting the first rays of the sun to signal the moment at which they would open. Exactly on time, a porter swung open the gates. This was no scurvy knave like the one who had caused trouble to Adam and Clym at Carlisle but a smart, well-dressed young man with a sergeant at his back. Trickery wouldn't have got them through these gates. But trickery was not needed and the four travellers surged through with nearly a hundred others who had been waiting.

Will had never seen such crowds and even the adults looked around in awe. It seemed that all the people in the world must be gathered in that small space but there was no time to waste gawping at the sights. Adam stopped a passer-by.

"Where can we find the king?"

"The king? What's the likes of you want with the king?"

"Just tell us where to find him, that's all."

"At the palace, of course."

"Where's that?"

"Westminster."

But before they could enquire the way to Westminster, the man had already hurried on his way. Adam was about to pursue him to teach him better manners but Clym put out a restraining hand.

"Leave it, Adam. We're not in Inglewood now. Best not to cause trouble when we're far from home. And you don't ken what friends he has."

"Did I hear you say 'Inglewood', friend?" said a voice.

The four travellers looked round to see a big, friendly-looking man in rough, country clothes. He was smiling broadly.

"Did I hear you say 'Inglewood'?" he said again. "I'm from Penrith. It's good to hear north country talk again."

"I did say 'Inglewood'," answered Clym. "We're from Carlisle. We're right glad to see a friendly face. We only arrived in London this morning."

"Then you must come and have a bite to eat. You look as if you need a meal and you can pay for it by telling me all the news."

"Please forgive us, my friend," said Adam. "We have messages for the king and we must seek him out at once or we shall be in trouble with our lord."

The stranger's smile vanished but before he could speak, Clym smiled and said, "We would fain talk with you, friend. Undoubtedly, you will have much to teach us about London and we were in Penrith only three weeks ago. We can bring you the news of home. Perhaps you will be our guest tonight. I am sure the king will reward us for our message and we can use the king's silver to buy us all a meal."

The stranger's smile returned.

"That's noble of you. But I made the offer first. We'll meet again after compline at the sign of the red cow in Cheapside. Anyone will direct you. So, farewell until we meet."

"Hold fast a moment," said Adam. "We're strangers here, as you know. Can you be so kind as to tell us where we may find the king? At the palace, we're told, but we don't ken where that is."

Their new friend struck his forehead with the heel of his hand. "Of course! How thoughtless of me! Come I'll bring you to the king's palace and show you Cheapside along the way. Come, young man, your father and his friends look tired and you look as if you could do with a lift."

And, so saying, he hoisted Will onto his shoulders and set off through a warren of streets and alleys. From his vantage point, Will could see almost into the upstairs windows of many of the houses but the stranger maintained such a pace that he found little time to wonder at the sights revealed and had to hang on tightly to his steed's head. Many of the houses were much like those to which they were accustomed in Carlisle but there were more of them and many of them were much grander and had guards on duty. On closer inspection, the people, though, were different.

Amongst the Saxons, there were men and women from all the king's dominions. The outlaws saw with dismay that there were many more Normans than at home. And, although they didn't recognise them all, there were Flemings, Gascons, Bretons and, even, (Will stared in wonder) a dark-visaged Moor but William, Adam and Clym had to keep their wits about them to keep up and avoid losing their guide in the crowded streets and at the various crossing places.

Their route was mainly down hill as they made their way towards the river but, for all its importance, London was still little more than a league across and it was not long before their guide, not pausing for breath, pointed to a street on their right – "Cheapside", he said, "but we mustn't keep the king waiting, must we?" – and he hurried on.

At length, after William and his friends had become thoroughly confused, their guide stopped. "There," he said, "is the palace."

In front of them, across a broad, open space, was the most splendid building that the northerners had ever seen. It seemed to stretch across the entire horizon and its walls appeared to reach upwards to heaven. It was guarded in front by soldiers in brightly-coloured apparel, and even more brightly dressed men and women on splendidly caparisoned horses were coming and going through the enormous entrance.

The palace seemed to shine in the early morning sun and from its upper stories flew many bright banners. Hawkers and chapmen tried to attract the attention of the fine ladies and gentlemen, and lumbering carts with solid wheels crunched across the stony ground before them. Some of the carts had brightly-coloured screens to protect the occupants from the gaze of passers-by but most were open and provided space for humans and baggage alike. Many were pulled by servants or their owners but others were drawn by horses or bullocks. At the entrance to the palace was a group of beggars with terrible injuries supporting themselves on home-made crutches – old soldiers from Louis' crusade.

"The guards won't let me in," said their friend, "so I won't come any nearer. You mun go on your own. I am sure you will have no difficulty when you show the guards your letters. May good luck go with you until we meet tonight. Remember: the sign of the red cow. Ask for Stephen." He turned and disappeared into the crowd.

CHAPTER SEVEN

> They preced prestly into the hall,
> Of no man had they dreade;
> The porter came after and dyd them call,
> And with them began to chyde.

"Now what?" asked Adam. "We've no letters. How do we get in? I don't think it's any good trying the trick I used in Carlisle with these people."

"We'll just have to be confident. We can say our message isn't written down because our lord was afraid it might get stolen. We'll have to say it's a spoken message."

"Will they believe us?"

"They'll have to. It's all we can do. If we say we have come to warn the king of treason, they'll be afraid that if we don't warn the king they'll get blamed and let us in. At least I hope so."

"We don't look like important messengers wearing these rags. They weren't so bad when we set out but they are much the worse for wear now."

"All the better. It looks like we we've been on the journey a long time."

"Well, that's true at least, but genuine messengers would have come on horse back."

"Only if we were messengers from a lord or a sheriff or someone. We won't mention any lord. We'll say we've heard people plotting and we've come to tell the king."

"Why didn't we tell the sheriff?"

"You could say it was the sheriff who was plotting, Da," said Will.

"The sheriff? How would the like of us hear the sheriff plotting?"

"It doesn't really matter," said Clym. "We just tell the guards we've heard the sheriff plotting and they won't dare refuse to let us in."

"And when we see the king? What do we tell him?"

"We tell him the truth. We won't get two chances. We throw

ourselves on his mercy and ask for pardon."

"Well, it's no good standing around. Let's go. Let me do the talking," said Adam.

Adam could talk a squirrel out of a tree, so no-one argued. With apparent confidence, the four of them crossed the palace forecourt towards the entrance gates. They felt as if the whole world was watching them and as if the distance across the forecourt was half a league instead of only a hundred paces. Will counted the steps and kept his head held high, looking, if anything, more confident than his father. Half way across, they saw a large party of finely-dressed horsemen accompanied by a crowd of servants on foot approaching the palace gates.

"Quick!" said Clym. "get behind this lot. If we stick close, they might think we're all together."

Without waiting to see if the others had understood, he increased his pace and edged almost between two of the servants at the back of the group. He was glad to see Adam, William and Will fall in with him. One of the servants looked a bit suspicious but Adam, as ever, thinking quickly, turned to him.

"I'm new with my master, friend. Which is yours?"

"The one in green on the big bay. The Lord Peter de Tilliol of Scaleby," responded the man and, then, suspiciously, "And which is your new master? I haven't seen you – or your friends – in our party before."

The thought that the servant's master was from Scaleby, only a few miles from Carlisle, alarmed Adam but he disguised his anxiety and said, "We only joined my master this morning. He wanted a bigger following – to impress the king, I think. They're all the same aren't they? See one lord with a dozen attendants and they mun have a dozen and a half. Have you been with your master long? To be honest with you, we only joined ours for the offer of a good meal and to get some new clothes. If we're lucky, that is. He'll probably kick us back where he found us once he's seen the king. Anyway, where's Scaleby? Can't say as I've heard of it. One of those places up north is it? He looks a kind master. Not like ours. I'm sure ours'd want every last labour of our bodies before he'd pay us. Anyway, like I say, I expect we'll be kicked back where we came from as soon as today's over."

Adam paused for breath. He would have prattled on for as long as it took to avoid having to answer the other's questions but his companion interrupted.

"And like *I* said, who is your master and where have you come from? You weren't of our number last night."

Adam was not going to be trapped into answering who his master was but he couldn't avoid the second question. The answer came in a moment of inspiration.

"We live at the sign of the red cow in Cheapside. It's a way over that way," he said gesturing vaguely behind him. And then, before the other could speak, he rattled on, "It's not much of a place but we help to look after the customers and even Little Dicon here helps out as pot boy."

He glanced down at 'Little Dicon', fearing he might renounce his new name but, possibly fortunately, Will was concentrating on looking confident and didn't hear. It was clear that de Tilliol's servant was about to say something more but, by now, the conversation had served its immediate purpose and had carried them passed the beggars and beyond the outer gates into the great courtyard. Adam looked round and, seeing the guards were occupied with some new arrivals, he pretended to stumble and allowed his companion to move a little ahead. He turned to William and Clym.

"Come on. We'll have to make a dash for it," he said. "That must be the door. Over there. Up those steps. Come on. Now!"

He turned and, with the others behind him, ran for the broad, stone staircase that led from the courtyard into the palace itself. Immediately, there was a shout of alarm as first one person and then another realised that something was amiss. Fortunately for them, the hubbub in the centre of the courtyard drew attention away from the three outlaws and Will who were already half way up the steps. Without pausing they passed through the doorway and rushed quickly passed the porter and into the hall. But there they came face to face with the usher who barred their way and the porter, who had been so unceremoniously ignored, came after them shouting and calling for the guards.

To have continued to force their way forward would have been fruitless and, indeed, dangerous and they stopped, facing the imposing, black-clad figure of the usher. Here was no bumpkin. The usher was an important functionary and he spoke quietly and with authority, conscious that guards and others were now present.

"Yeomen, what is the meaning of this, I pray? Would you disgrace the king's officers? Good sirs, where are you from?"

Even Adam could detect the mockery in the phrase 'good sirs' but, sensing that only honesty would serve, he answered directly.

"Sir, without any falsehood, we're outlaws of the forest and we have come here to see our king and petition for his pardon," he said quietly.

As he spoke, there occurred one of those pauses in general conversation which resulted in everyone within the room hearing his words. Adam had not seen the king and queen who were sitting on a dais at the far end of the room. Now he saw the sturdily built, but imposing, figure of King Henry II who stared at him with his grey eyes from under his short, red hair.

The king was only twenty-five years old but he'd already acquired the manner of command and seemed to Adam to carry all the authority of a god. The silence deepened yet further as the king looked up. The queen, Eleanor of Aquitaine, with her greater age, the experience of the French court and travel with her former husband, Louis VII, on the Crusades, looked even more stern and unapproachable. All around, courtiers and servants alike stared at Adam and his friends. Even the king's hounds seemed to have ceased their quarrelling and to be watching too. The usher, however, was too experienced to allow the embarrassing silence to cause him obvious discomfort.

"What? Outlaws? What impertinence is this? Ho! Guards! Take these men. Remove them from the king's presence and keep them fast in the guardhouse until the king's pleasure be known."

The king raised his hand and, in a quiet voice which nevertheless carried to all parts of the hall, commanded, "Hold a minute, Master Usher. These men interest me. Bring them before me."

"You heard the king's command. Bring them forward, guards, to the king's presence."

The guards, who now surrounded the outlaws, moved forward and grasped them firmly, but not roughly, by the arms, two to each man.

"What about me?" asked Will.

"You come along, too," said one of the soldiers.

"Don't you want to hold me?"

"Don't be cheeky, you young whelp. Just you come along and no impertinence."

With the usher leading the way, the three outlaws and six soldiers, with Will bringing up the rear, walked the length of the hall in a ragged procession to where the king and queen sat.

"Down on your knees, as the law requires."

The four of them knelt down as instructed and each of the three adults lifted up his hands in homage. Will, watching, copied the adults after a moment's pause.

Before the king could speak, Adam, knowing he may not have another chance, said, "Lord, we beseech you to grant us pardon for slaying your deer..."

He would have continued but "Silence!" thundered the usher. "You may not speak until the king gives you leave."

The king, too, held silence as if the usher's command was directed also at him. He held a long, unwavering stare and then said, "Tell me your names." And, when they appeared to hesitate, "At once."

"Adam Bell."

"Clym of the Clough."

"William of Cloudesley."

"Will, if it pleases Your Majesty."

"Silence, child!" said the king. And, then, turning to the adults,

"Are you those thieves that men have told me of? I here make a vow to God. You shall be hanged, all three. As I am king of this land, you shall be executed without mercy. Arrest them!"

The soldiers, moved forward again and, seizing the three outlaws, dragged them to their feet and waited the king's command to remove them.

"My Lord," cried out Adam desperately, "we beseech you to grant us pardon. We gave ourselves up to you of our free will. Grant us, then, freedom to leave here with our weapons and if we live for a hundred years we will ask no more pardon." And he again attempted to throw himself on the floor at the king's feet.

"You speak proudly," said the king, "but all three of you shall be hanged. Take them away."

"Hold a moment!" The queen, who had so far kept silent, spoke. "It would be a great pity to hang such stout yeomen if it were possible to pardon them with honour. My Lord," she said, turning to the king, "when I first came into this land to be your wife, you said you would grant me the first boon that I should ask of you. All these years I have never asked such a boon. Therefore, my Lord, grant it to me now."

"Then ask it, madam, and I will grant it."

"Then, my good Lord, I like these men. Give them to me."

"Madam," said the king, "You might have asked for a boon worth more than these three men. You could have asked for towers or towns or parks or forests – as much as you wanted."

"But none so pleasant or dear to me, my Lord."

"Madam, since that is your wish, your wish shall be granted but I would rather have given you three good market towns."

The queen was pleased and thanked the king. "Lord, I thank you. I dare undertake for them that they will be true to you henceforward. But, good my Lord, speak unto them, some kind word that they might be comforted."

The king hesitated but, thinking his reputation for magnanimity demanded some suitable gesture from him, said, "I grant you pardon. Now, fellows, go wash and join my company at meat."

Adam and his friends bowed deeply before the king and queen and were about to thank him when the usher, seeing their intention, ordered, "Silence, rogues. You have been dismissed. Do not address the king again," and signed to the soldiers to lead them away. The crowds parted to give them passage but, when they arrived at the bottom of the hall among the servants, everyone gathered round to congratulate them, eager to hear their story.

CHAPTER EIGHT

>They had not setten but a whyle,
>Certayne without lesynge,
>There came messengers out of the north,
>With letters to our kynge.

The story telling had scarce begun when there was a disturbance that interrupted their conversation. A large company of persons arrived at the door and were confronted by the usher. Adam was alarmed to see the Lord of Scaleby at their head.

"Trouble," he whispered to Clym.

"How so?"

"It's the lord of Scaleby. Come, perhaps, to tell the king about us."

Before Adam and Clym could discuss the matter and even before Clym could pass the news to William, the usher met the new arrivals and, clearly recognising them as important, conducted them immediately to the king. The newcomers kneeled before him.

"My lord," said de Tilliol, "your officers of Carlisle in the north country humbly greet you."

"You are right welcome," replied the king. "Ho! You boy! Bring wine for my loyal servants. They must refresh themselves after their long journey. Make room, my lords, for my good friends."

There was a general shuffling about as those at the king's table made room for the newcomers and some gave up their stools. Although de Tilliol had visited London when his manor had been restored to him and he'd sworn fealty, it was clear to those with the king that His Majesty didn't recognise his visitors – Scaleby and, indeed, Carlisle were a long way from London and visitors from the north weren't regular members of the court. Nevertheless, he made de Tilliol welcome and, then, to cover his lapse of memory, turned to his usher.

"Announce these lords to the company so that all may know them."

The usher bent to speak to de Tilliol and then mounted the dais and, in a loud voice announced, "His Majesty has welcomed the Lord Peter de Tilliol of Scaleby in Cumberland and bids all present do him and his company likewise."

THEY HAD NOT SETTEN BUT A WHYLE

De Tilliol stood and bowed to the assembly.

William nudged Clym, "Did you hear that?" he whispered. "It's the Lord of Scaleby. He's bound to have brought messages from Carlisle."

"Aye, it's likely, but not certain. He might be here for some other reason. I've heard he has lands in the south country. Mayhap he's not been in Carlisle recently. Anyway, the king's pardoned us. We'll be all right."

While they were whispering together, the king spoke to de Tilliol, who had not seated himself after bowing to the company.

"How fares my justice and my sheriff of Carlisle?"

"Sir, without a lie, they are slain. And many officers more."

"Slain? How so? Who has done this? Tell me at once."

"Three outlaws. Adam Bell, Clym of the Clough and William of Cloudesley."

"Say you so? It grieves me to hear it. I would rather have known this an hour ago than have a thousand pounds, for I have just pardoned them. If I had known this before, I would have hanged all three of them. You have a letter? With details? Show me."

De Tilliol bowed again and handed over the letter he'd brought from Carlisle.

Henry tore open the letter and read it slowly. He spoke many languages – indeed people said he spoke all languages from the French sea to Jordan – and knew law and history but he still found reading difficult. Now, he was too impatient to await the help of a clerk and struggled with the well rounded and elaborate phrases of the Latin. The scribes in Carlisle had worked with care to maximise the shocking the events of that day when Adam and his friends had escaped from the city but had striven to disguise the failures of the city authorities, most blame being assigned to the dead justice and sheriff. Eventually, his face red with anger, Henry spoke.

"I read here of three hundred men slain! The mayor, the sheriff, the justice, all the constables and catchpoles, the bailiffs, the beadles, the sergeants-at-law and forty foresters. Slain by three outlaws! How is this possible, my Lord of Scaleby?"

He was in a towering rage, the veins in his neck standing out purple against the now livid colour of his normally healthy complexion. Henry in a rage was something even his closest friends feared and de Tilliol realised he had provoked a storm which might unleash its fury on him, the messenger.

"My Liege," he said, kneeling and bowing so low his head almost touched the ground, "I have no details other than those in the letter that was read to me before it was sealed. I was not in Carlisle. Indeed, I was not on my manor of Scaleby but was visiting neighbours to the east. The men of quality are all dead as you see and it was left to the prior of Carlisle to provide this intelligence for Your Majesty."

"It says that these outlaws have trespassed in my parks and slain my deer. It says that no more dangerous men walk the land to east or west. What? Why not north and south? What else have these men done? Why were they not apprehended ere this? How have they escaped to come here and see me in my capital of London?"

De Tilliol remained on his knee. "My liege, I crave your indulgence. This was a matter for the sheriff and as you see he cannot now answer for his failure. My manor is to the east of Carlisle and Inglewood, the home of these outlaws is to the south and west. Moreover, my liege, I visit my manor only when my leisure permits. As Your Majesty recalls, it was only last year that Your Majesty graciously returned the honour to me after Your Majesty received Cumberland from King Malcolm."

Henry was pleased to be reminded of his diplomatic skills in obtaining the return of his northern territories so peacefully but he was still angry.

"Take up the tables," he ordered, "for I will eat no more."

De Tilliol and his party had not eaten but were, perforce, compelled to watch as the tables were cleared of victuals and wine. The king rose. His love of sport now stood Adam and his friends, no longer outlaws, in good stead. As Clym had said, Henry was a fair man and, despite his anger, he couldn't in honour revoke the pardon he had granted. Henry was also a keen sportsman and he now called for his best archers to come forward and to go with him to the butts.

"I will see these fellows, who have brought the north country into so much woe, shoot against my best bowmen. Let us see how good they really are."

"My liege," said Queen Eleanor, "pray allow my archers also to be tried."

"Of course, of course," he responded impatiently.

The king, as ever, wasted no more time in discussion and, not pausing to allow his courtiers to prepare themselves, led the way from the palace to the stables where he mounted his horse, without which he was seldom seen outdoors, and rode quickly away in the direction of the open country on the edge of the city at Finsbury Fields. Archers, courtiers and others keen to see the sport hurried alongside or trailed behind, struggling to keep pace.

News of the presence of the king and queen seemed to travel like wildfire and crowds pressed closely in the narrow streets, cheering the royal party and jostling to get a good view. Soldiers kept them at a distance with crossed pikes but the crowd was good-natured and the soldiers, too, saw no need for aggression. But the crowds slowed progress and when they arrived at the butts, there was a further delay while the targets were set up and the archers prepared themselves.

Just before everything was ready, Henry, as always, too impatient to wait, rode off with his squire and his hawk causing yet more confusion for his long-suffering staff but, fortuitously, giving time for Queen Eleanor and her ladies, escorted by her company of archers to arrive. Eleanor was carried in a litter as it was well known she was expecting her fifth child later in the year.

Adam, Clym and William, bemused by all the new experiences and dazzled by the splendid crowd, stood around watching the comings and goings of the soldiers, archers, courtiers and townspeople. They had scarcely become accustomed to their good fortune.

"It was lucky we got here before de Tilliol," said William.

"Aye. And lucky the queen prevailed on the king to pardon us. He wasn't even going to listen to us. Why do you think she took our side?" asked Clym.

"I reckon she took a fancy to William," said Adam. "Did you see the look she gave him?"

"Hush! Don't make jokes like that! Someone'll hear you and then we'll be in trouble again," said William.

"I'm not so sure it was a joke. She was giving you quite a look. Just like you. All the maids in Carlisle'd be after you if Alys didn't keep her eye out."

"Hold your peace! The queen wouldn't be interested in a Saxon – even if he was a lord. Anyway, the best bit of luck was the king. When he read de Tilliol's letter I thought it was all up for us even if he had pardoned us. Why didn't he change his mind and have us arrested again?"

"I reckon there were two things," said Clym. "He wouldn't want to break his word to the queen and he wanted to see how we can shoot. He's a true soldier and wants to see the people who killed three hundred men on their own!"

"But it wasn't true. We didn't kill anything like three hundred men," protested Adam.

"The king doesn't ken that. I reckon we're lucky to have Master Sureshot here with us – even if we lose him to Her Majesty before bed-time."

The banter continued but, for them, as much as for Will, the scene provided plenty at which to wonder and, the four of them watched the activity with undisguised interest. The butts had been set up long before the king returned in the early afternoon. Amongst the colourful crowd, he was almost drab. Despite the hot sun, he wore his usual short cloak over what, on anyone else, would be ordinary working clothes and these, now, were spattered with grime after his hunting. But his commanding presence and handsome features ensured he wouldn't be mistaken for any lesser person.

"What? Are you not ready yet?" he called as he came. He seemed to have recovered some of his earlier good humour and there was no malice in his voice.

"He only went hawking to make things difficult for everyone else," muttered a bystander before he noticed Will gazing at him and hurriedly moved away.

Now that the king had returned, it was a matter of moments before the first marksmen were lining up for the contest. Each man shot three times, the king's men first, then the queen's archers and, finally, Adam, William and Clym. In the first round almost everyone hit the target without difficulty – except one of the king's men who was jeered off the field. The king provided a replacement and the butts were moved back fifty paces. The distance was more of a challenge this time and several men missed with at least one arrow. All three former outlaws hit the target with all their shafts.

Another fifty paces and misses became more frequent but still most hit the targets. When the butts were moved yet another fifty paces, the misses became more frequent than the hits. Even Clym missed with one arrow and a howl of derision went up not withstanding that several of the royal archers had missed with two arrows and one had missed with all three.

"They want us to lose," snarled the usually peaceful Clym.

At the next length only two of the royal archers remained but Adam, William and Clym all hit the targets.

"That'll show them," growled a somewhat mollified Clym.

Then William spoke in a loud voice.

"By Him who died for me, I hold him no archer who shoots at butts so wide."

"Whereat should men shoot?" demanded the king. "I pray you tell me."

"At such a butt, sir, as men use in my country as by your leave I will show Your Majesty!" and, on the king's signal, he went into the field with Adam and Clym and set up two hazel rods four hundred paces apart. Standing by the nearer rod he said, "I hold him an archer, that yonder wand cleaves in two."

"There is none such here," said the king, "nor none else that can do so."

"I will try, sir, before I do ought else."

William carefully selected a bearing arrow from his quiver. This was a special, long and stiff arrow with small fletchings to reduce drag and intended for great distances. William held it in his hand, sighting along its length to ensure it was straight and true.

"Good luck, brother," said Adam. "It's a goodly distance."

"William's done as much afore today, and there's no wind." said Clym. "But good fortune be with you," he said, turning to William.

William stepped up to the mark, fitted the arrow and drew his bow. The crowd fell quiet. William appeared almost to take no aim and loosed his shaft. In the silence, the arrow hummed towards the distant hazel rod ... and split it in two.

A sigh went up from the crowd and then a cheer. The king called William to his side. "Now, fellow, thou art the best archer that I ever saw," he said.

"And yet, by your leave, sire, I will do more," said William. "I have here a son who is seven years old and who is very dear to me. I will tie him to a stake for all here to see. And I will place an apple on his head. I will go six score paces from him and, with a broad arrow, I will cleave the apple in two."

Henry stared, conscious that all those nearby had heard the boast. If he was not pleased to have this arrogant outlaw making mockery of his archers, he was much less pleased to have him, as he thought, making mockery of him. "Well then, fellow, make haste. Do as you say. But, by Him who died on the Cross, if you do not do as you boast, I'll have you hanged. And, if you touch a hair of his head, or even his gown, then, by all the saints in heaven, I'll hang all three of you."

"That which I have promised," said William, "I never will forswear."

A stake was brought and William drove it into the earth right there before the king. The crowd, suddenly aware that some special feat was to be attempted, but not yet sure what, pressed round. William bound Will to the stake facing the king.

"Now, Will. you're a brave lad. You ken I can hit the apple but you mun hold still and not move even a little bit. I've turned you this way so you won't flinch when I shoot."

"I won't flinch, anyway. You ken that."

"I know. But it's best to be sure."

"I am sure."

"Well. It's always best to be sure!"

William set the apple on Will's head and paced out six score paces.

Henry's squire walked with him to check the distance. "You're a fool, stranger. His Majesty didn't need any more proof of your skill. He saw what you can do with the hazel wand. Anyway, the distance is not so great this time."

"But I am using a broad arrow this time. It's heavier for the distance."

"Aye. And it can do more damage. You had best not hit the king, if you value your life. Well, God guide your shaft."

Adam handed William his great war bow and Clym helped him to choose a good, broad arrow that was newly fletched, stiff and strong.

"That one'll do," said Clym. "It's good and straight. As true a shaft as you ever fashioned. God be with you. Or, rather, God be with young Will."

"Go to Will for me, Clym. Stand where he can see you."

Clym hastened to do as asked, feeling guilty that he hadn't thought to go to Will before being asked.

"Although it's William should be looking to his son, not me," he thought.

The crowd had, by now, realised the feat that was to be undertaken and pressed close about.

"Give the fellow room," called the squire, acting as herald on what was, still, an informal occasion. "Stand back. Stand back. His Majesty must see the shot."

The crowd withdrew somewhat but there was still an excited and distracting buzz of conversation as people argued over the shot. Many people were openly betting on the outcome but others prayed for William, that his life might be saved and that he wouldn't harm Will.

"He's a brave lad, for certain."

"The father's a fool."

"Or a knave."

"He's an arrogant swine."

"He'd best not miss. The king won't stand for that."

Many women were overcome by the danger and were weeping with anxiety and, then, people seemed suddenly to recognise that William was about to shoot towards them and hastily drew away from the vicinity of the stake to which William was tied. The king, though nearer than most, stood his ground, not willing to appear afraid and not willing to allow a mere Saxon to seem to have the steadier nerve. Queen Eleanor stayed beside the king, still mounted on his horse, and the principal courtiers, perforce, also remained near although nervously shuffling about trying to get others between them and William.

"My lords and good friends," called William, "pray be silent for me and still. He who shoots for such a wager needs quiet so he can take his aim. Quiet please."

He stepped up to the mark and, on the king's signal, he nocked his arrow and drew his bow and, for once, paused on the draw to settle his aim and wait briefly as a zephyr of wind disturbed the grasses. The bow was so strong that many a man would have had difficulty in making a full draw but William's strength was such that his arm never wavered.

There was an involuntary gasp from the crowd as the arrow loosed and then silence as everyone watched it speed to the target on Will's head. It was obvious to these expert spectators that William had the skill that was needed but everyone also understood the special nerve that was required for him to shoot a target so close to his son's head.

It needed luck, too, as even the tiniest puff of a vagrant breeze could send the arrow off course with fatal results for Will, William, Adam and Clym. But the thoughts were barely formulated in people's minds when there was a gasp and a roar of approval as the apple shattered. Will, who had, until that moment, held quite still slumped slightly in his bonds but then straightened up again and held himself erect and as still as before. Clym ran to him and hugged him tightly. Then he quickly undid the bonds and helped him towards where King Henry sat immovably on his horse.

Six score paces away Adam grasped William's hand.

"Well done. Now you mun go to the king."

William handed Adam his bow and walked steadily towards the king. The crowd was now silent again waiting to see Henry's reaction. William bowed low. For a moment the king thought, perhaps, that William was being impertinent but, then, he realised that even so arrogant a man must be relieved not to have injured his own son. He appreciated the feat and recognised that he must not appear churlish before his people. A king must behave as a king.

"May God forbid," he said, "that you should ever shoot at me."

A loud laugh, comprised partly of released tension and partly of appreciation of the king's humour, broke from the crowd and then everyone clapped and cheered again. When the noise had subsided, the king spoke again.

"Cloudesley, you shall be my personal bowman, you shall carry my bow and you will receive eighteen pence a day. Also you shall be my Chief Ranger of the north country. How say you?"

"My liege," said William, bowing low, "I am yours to command."

"By God and by my faith, and I will give you twelve pence a day," said Queen Eleanor. "Come and fetch thy payment when thou wilt. No man shall prevent thee. William, I make thee gentleman of clothing and of fee and thy two brothers shall be yeomen of my chamber for they please me also. And your son, because he is so young, shall work in my wine cellar until he comes of man's estate when he shall be advanced. And William, bring thy wife to London. I long to see her. She shall be my chief gentlewoman and govern the nursery."

William and the others were overwhelmed at the queen's graciousness and thanked Their Majesties with proper humility. The king and queen, however, scarcely waiting for thanks, turned away and busied themselves with their courtiers and, as was proper, left the job of ensuring that the erstwhile outlaws knew how to conduct themselves to others. Of course, even in their new status, they were still lowly and it was the humble people of the household who gathered round to offer their congratulations at their change in fortune.

When they were alone once more, it was Clym who spoke first.

"Never do anything like that again. I know you're a good shot and can hit a groat at two hundred paces, but it was wrong to take a chance with Will's life. There was no need. What would Alys have said? And what about Adam's life and mine? I heard what the king said."

Adam came to William's rescue. "Leave it be Clym. All's well. We're pardoned and have good jobs for life if we only take care for our manners. Will and Alys, too. I told you the queen fancied you, William. Gentleman of clothing and of fee forsooth! Where's the Saxon yeoman now?"

"Nay, it was you and Clym she said wanted for yeomen of her chamber because you 'pleased' her. Forsooth yourself!"

"Don't talk like that, even in jest," cautioned Clym. Someone may hear you and then we'd be in worse trouble than we were before. The queen's an honourable lady with young children and we owe her our lives. It's shame to talk so. And anyway, we haven't congratulated the real hero. Young Will, here, stood still while you shot arrows at him. Well done, young Will."

"Not 'young' Will," said Will. "Adam says I am a man now. You mun call me Will."

"And so I shall, Will. So I shall. And so shall all of us. But, come, we mun find the red cow in Cheapside and thank our friend from this morning."

It was as they were lying on their palliasses that night that William said, "We mun go to Rome to be absolved of our sins by the Pope."

Adam and Clym ignored this but it is recorded that the four of them did, indeed, travel to Rome where they received the blessings of the Holy Father – but that is another story. It only remains to say that they returned to dwell with the king and died good men all three.

****

Thus endeth the lives of these good yemen,
God send them eternall blysse,
And all that with hande bowe shoteth,
That of heaven may never mysse!

POSTSCRIPT

It would be a pity if anyone who has read *Outlaws of Inglewood* were to be misled into thinking that it is no more than just a simple story. It is, indeed, just a story – but it is not simple.

THE MEDIEVAL ORIGIN

The earliest reference of any kind to Adam Bell, Clym of the Clough and William of Cloudesley is in a parliamentary return for Wiltshire written in 1432 which includes, presumably as a joke, a sequence of outlaws' names, slightly disguised, including those of Adam Bell, William of Cloudesley and Clym of the Clough as well as those of Robin Hood, Little John, and Much the Miller's son.

It is clear, therefore, that the names of Adam Bell and his associates were known in Wiltshire by 1432 at the latest and one can infer that, for the outlaws' names to be worth using so far from the north country, the legend must have been current for some time. This particular reference provides a last possible date for the origin of the legend.

Our knowledge of the legend itself derives from a series of ballads dating from the sixteenth century, the most important of which, printed about 1565, serves as the basis for *Outlaws of Inglewood.*

The first of the ballads, dating from about 1510, exists only as a fragment of a longer text. It comprises of some 236 lines of text and may have been printed by Wynken de Worde (fl.1477–1535) who inherited Caxton's press on the latter's death in 1491. Assuming the date and attribution to be correct, it is among some of the earliest books to be printed in England.

The second ballad dates from 1536 and was from the press of John Bydell. It is also a fragment, and of rather fewer lines than the earlier text – only 94.

The third text, which is the earliest apparently more or less complete version, dates from 1565 or perhaps earlier and was published by William Copland (or Copeland) under the title *Adambel, Clym of the cloughe, and Wyllyam of cloudesle* and is now in the British Museum.

Other versions of the legend were registered with the Stationers'

POSTSCRIPT

Company in 1557-8 and in 1582. Later, in 1586, the Stationers' Company records mention another text as having been 'never printed before'. This version has not been certainly identified although Child tentatively links it with *The Second Part of Adam Bell*.

This story, sometimes known as *Young Cloudesley* from its having been included under that name (actually *Younge Cloudeslee*) in the Percy Folio, is regarded with disdain by modern scholars. Nonetheless, it is only very slightly later than the primary text and offers a name for William's eldest son – William, the diminutive of which is adopted in *Outlaws of Inglewood*.

Young Cloudesley, a story of some 111 four-line stanzas, is set near Mansfield and tells the romantic history of 'Yong William' who is in love with 'a bonny maide' called Cicely (spelled several different ways in different stanzas). Cicely is in love with another man, 'a stout and sturdie man ... of quality and kind' and rejects Will's suit but he tricks her into meeting him and kidnaps her. Cicely's lover eventually discovers her whereabouts and he and Will fight for two hours. Rangers try to part them but Will kills both them and Cicely's lover.

Will takes Cicely to a cave where they hide but the country is raised and a promise is given that the one who finds the fugitive will be made lord of Mansfield. William of Cloudesley, Adam Bell and Clym go to London to seek pardon for Will from the king but the king refuses and threatens to hang all four of them. The three former outlaws flee to the woods and the king raises a party of fifty thousand men to seek them out.

Outlawed again, the three apparently outwit the search party and the king, impressed with their prowess, reverses his policy and pardons them. At first the outlaws are suspicious of the king's true intent but Will goes to him and is reassured. The four men re-enter the king's service and Cicely comes alone to the court where she is welcomed by the queen who appoints her to be her lady in waiting although it is not clear whether she ever married Will.

At least twenty-five editions of the Adam Bell legend were printed over the next two hundred and fifty years in, for example, London, Newcastle, Paisley, Edinburgh, Stirling, Glasgow, Falkirk and, by Anthony Soulby, in Penrith. This last is now in Chetham's Library in Manchester. Another edition, a copy of which is now in the Bodleian Library, was printed and sold by Ann Bell of Penrith in 1805.

POSTSCRIPT

In the eighteenth century, Thomas Percy published (1765) his *Reliques of Ancient English Poetry*, a collection of ballads, sonnets and songs. Amongst these was the Copland (1565) version of the legend, but including 'corrections' derived from the so-called *Percy Folio*, a manuscript collection of ballad material in a 17th century hand now in the British Museum. Later, in 1791, Joseph Ritson (1752-1803) published his *Pieces of Ancient Popular Poetry* in which he included Copland's edition of the Adam Bell legend. It was Ritson's version which Francis Child (1825-96) used as the basis of his 1861 version and it is this that provides the main source for *Outlaws of Inglewood*.

THE LITERARY HERITAGE

Adam Bell, Clym of the Clough or William of Cloudesley are mentioned in a number of other contexts from the late sixteenth century onwards, sometimes in passing, but also as a major theme.

Child noted in 1861 that Shakespeare's *Much Ado about Nothing* (1598-9) contains a reference to Adam Bell in Act 1 Scene 1 in which Benedick says to Don Pedro, "If I do [fall in love], hang me in a bottle like a cat and shoot at me; and he that hits me, let him be clapped on the shoulder, and called Adam".

Robin Hood's Birth, Breeding, Valour and Marriage, of which at least three versions apparently survive from the seventeenth century, includes a reference to the Inglewood outlaws. In this ballad, the author has Adam Bell, William of Clowdeslé and Clim of the Clugh (*sic*) involved in an archery contest with Robin Hood's father. The contest, arranged by the Pinder of Wakefield, was for a prize of forty marks (£26.66). Robin's father was reputed to shoot "a lusty long bow, two north country miles and an inch at a shot" and he beat all three of our outlaws. Sadly, some modern scholars regard it as dating from no earlier than the Restoration in 1660.

Act 1 of Ben Jonson's *The Alchemist* (1610) includes an allusion to the Adam Bell legend when one of the characters says, "I bring you no cheating Clim o' the Cloughs, or Claribels".

Sir William Davenant's *The Long Vacation in London* (1673) mentions "Adam Bell and Clymme" and in about 1831, William Wordsworth referred to the outlaws in his sonnet *Suggested by a View from an Eminence in Inglewood Forest* (see introductory pages).

POSTSCRIPT

It seems that, before the present volume, only one novelisation of the legend had appeared: that of Pierce Egan the Younger (1814 – 1880), a prolific author of adventure stories, who wrote an account of the legend in a series of weekly instalments completed in 1842 for the publishing firm of Hextall and Wall and which was later published in book form under the title *Adam Bell, Clym o' the Cleugh and William of Cloudeslie* in the same year.

Egan's story, typical of early Victorian wordiness, is one of 190 closely-set pages of which the first 153 have no connection with the medieval legend apart from the names of some of the principal protagonists. In this part of the novel, the Alys of *Outlaws* is introduced as Guillelmine, the niece and ward of 'Jude le Trompeur', baron and lord of Carlisle castle. She adopts the name 'Alice' after her marriage to William in order that she can live undetected in Carlisle.

In 1883, that most influential of American illustrator/authors of adventure fiction, Howard Pyle (1853-1911), describes in his story, *The Merry Adventures of Robin Hood of Great Renown in Nottinghamshire* how Little John and Robin Hood first met and has Little John compare Robin Hood's skill with a bow with that of Adam Bell.

" 'Now by the lusty yew bow of good Saint Withold,' cried the stranger, 'that is a shot indeed, and never saw I the like in all my life before! Now truly will I be thy man henceforth and for aye. Good Adam Bell was a fair shot, but never shot he so!' "

Occasional publications during the twentieth century include accounts of the Adam Bell legend including, apparently, Jose Manuel Carbonell's *La Cenicienta* (Cinderella) published in 1963. It was also included in Jennifer Westwood's *Tales and Legends* (1971). Although presented as a story for children, it was a useful version for adults because, although a free translation and with a degree of sanitisation, it was the only available modern English edition until the more accurate version by Hahn. The story was also included in Roderick Hunt's *Myths and Legends*, one of the junior readers published by the Oxford University Press.

A 1983 episode of the HTV-Goldcrest television series *Robin of Sherwood* was devoted to Adam Bell. In this story by Anthony Horowitz, Adam Bell (played by Bryan Marshall), is seen as an elderly outlaw who captures Martin, the sheriff's nephew. The sheriff is holding Much the Miller's son captive and Robin agrees to help the sheriff to rescue his nephew in return for the release of Much. An elaborate story develops in which Adam, who turns out to be an admirer of Robin, saves Robin's life.

1992 saw the publication of *Lady of the Forest*, Jennifer Roberson's lengthy and innovative account of the early life of Maid Marion and of her meeting with Robin Hood. It is innovative, not in its being a complete invention owing little to the original ballads – it shares this with most other versions of Robin Hood – but in that it focuses on the story from the woman's perspective and that it has a robust adult tone that is very different from the usual Byronic fantasies for children. In this story, Adam Bell and his two friends are introduced as minor characters who reappear periodically as outlaws of Sherwood Forest.

'Cousins' of 5 October 1993(?), an electronic 'fanzine' for those interested in the religious and occult elements of the *Robin of Sherwood* television series, gives what appears to be an extract from a longer story apparently by Hilda Marshall in which 'Abbot Hugo' and his brother, Robert, the sheriff of Nottingham, are holding Adam Bell captive. After some time spent taunting Adam, Hugo and the sheriff free Adam in order to avoid making him a martyr.

As remarked above, some of these references are merely allusions to the characters in the legend, but others use them as a major theme. However, few of these latter owe much to the original, 16th century ballad, merely demonstrating a continuing interest in the legend.

The link with Robin Hood is not surprising. Outlaws, venison, skilled archery, the greenwood, the north country and the similar language of the ballads combine to make the idea inevitable. It is significant, or perhaps just curious, that there is a degree of unanimity that Adam Bell was somewhat older than Robin Hood. However, despite the work of Phillips and Keatman, Hunter, Holt and others, no evidence has ever been produced that can be accepted as showing that Robin Hood was a single, real person. Any attempt to suggest a chronology for the Adam Bell story based on Robin Hood's existence seems, therefore, to be doomed to failure.

POSTSCRIPT

THE HISTORICAL REFERENCES

In July 1575, Queen Elizabeth I was the guest at Kenilworth of Robert Earl of Leicester. Among the entertainment provided were a number of stories and songs including ones about Robin Hood and Adam Bell, Clym of the Clough and William of Cloudesley .

In *The Arte of English Poesie*, attributed to the 16th century writer, George Puttenham, the author exemplifies *Adam Bell* and *Clymme of the Clough* when discussing rhyme in poetry but dismisses the ballad as popular music such as stories of old time made for the recreation of 'common people' in 'tauernes, alehouses and such other places of base resort'.

In his *Original Chronicle of Scotland* written in about 1420 Andrew Wyntoun places Robin Hood and Little John in Inglewood in about 1283. Whilst not mentioning 'our' outlaws, it does reinforce the notion of a link with the Robin Hood legends made in *Robin Hood's Birth, Breeding, Valour and Marriage* and, perhaps, provides a degree of support to those other stories which link the two outlaw bands directly. The link of the Robin Hood legend to Inglewood is also implied by William Dunbar, the Scottish poet (c1465-c1530), who, in his poem *Of Sir Thomas Norray*, mentions one 'Allane Bell' in association with 'Gy of Gyfburne' (Guy of Gisborne), Robin Hood's adversary. Several modern scholars believe that Allane Bell and Adam Bell are the same person.

A strange historical connection is the presence in St Mary's Church, Bromsberrow of a stained glass window in the Yate Chapel depicting Adam Bell and William of Cloudeslee (*sic*) in separate panels. Quite why a church in Gloucestershire should depict Cumbrian outlaws is unclear but, apparently, much of the glass in the Yate Chapel was brought to Bromsberrow by a former rector, the Reverend H.G.D. Yate from Quedgeley Manor, of which he was then the owner, in about 1781. The glass is believed to be 17th century and of Flemish origin. The outlaws are figured in the outer two of three lower panels of which the central depicts a landscape of trees and the silhouette of a man (Clym of the Clough?) walking. Some of the other glass in the window, which appears to be something of a hotch-potch, seems to have been taken from Llanthony Priory to Quedgeley at the time of the Dissolution but there appears to be no reason to suppose that the glass depicting the outlaws had this origin – although the priory at Carlisle and that at Llanthony were both Augustinian.

WAS THE STORY BASED ON REAL HISTORY?

As has happened with Robin Hood, it is not surprising that the idea that Adam Bell, William of Cloudesley and Clym of the Clough may have been historical persons has been suggested, especially by Victorian antiquarians. But it has to be said that there is not any, even moderately, convincing evidence to support this thesis. Joseph Hunter provided the least unsatisfactory argument to support the idea in his two volume work *New Illustrations of the Life, Studies, and Writings of Shakespeare*. But his work does not withstand careful scrutiny. Child says, "it must be confessed that Mr Hunter is easily satisfied". Other, modern, authors have been less charitable and Dobson and Taylor regard Hunter's efforts to identify an historical Adam Bell as "extraordinarily unconvincing".

Members of Clan Bell, however, believe that there is a record of an Adam Bell, an archer living in the forest near Carlisle, in 1178. If this can be demonstrated, the individual concerned must, surely, be the Adam Bell of the legend. The assignment of so exact a date suggests authenticity but, unfortunately, all efforts to trace this record to its source have been unavailing.

THE HISTORICAL SETTING

If documentary evidence is lacking, is it possible to make the assumption that the ballad of Adam Bell is true and to draw conclusions as to date from that? Probably not. But let us briefly examine the possibilities.

It seems that, prior to the overlordship of King David and King Malcolm IV, the fortifications of Carlisle were rudimentary. Although the fortification of the city had been ordered by William I in 1072 and again by William II in 1092, very little had been done until David I of Scotland completed the stone walls and keep. David and, later, Malcolm IV then held the castle and it was not until its restoration to England by the Treaty of Chester in 1157 that any English king had effective sovereignty over a fully fortified Carlisle. A fortified castle and town is necessary because William of Cloudesley was ordered to

POSTSCRIPT

be cast into the deepest dungeon and because substantial walls were needed through which the swineherd could escape the city and in which there would have been strongly constructed gates to close against the outlaws. It seems, then, that the events of the story took place after 1157.

The ballad says that William was outlawed for poaching deer. Admittedly, the term 'outlaw' was often used casually but, until the Charter of the Forests, promulgated in 1217 during the regency of the early years of Henry III's reign, the punishment for poaching was either maiming or death. After 1217, whilst it is certainly true that William would have been likely to suffer hanging for killing townspeople during his arrest when his house was fired, he would not have been executed for poaching. Moreover, the Charter specifically abolished outlawry for killing the king's deer and released from their outlawry, without legal proceedings, all those who had been outlawed for a forest offence only. He would not, then, sensibly, have been willing to risk killing people to escape imprisonment or a fine which were, by then, the punishments he might have expected. This suggests that the events of the legend must have occurred before 1217.

We have three adult kings between 1157 and 1217 who might have been the king of the legend: Henry II (1154 – 1189), Richard I (1189 – 1199) and John (1199 – 1216).

Richard can be dismissed from consideration because his queen, Berengaria, never visited England.

King John (1199 – 1216) married the Countess of Gloucester in 1189, ten years before his accession to the throne, but the marriage was annulled in 1200 and there was no issue to justify the Queen in the ballad appointing Alys to be governor of the nursery. John married, a second time, to the twelve year old Isabella of Angoulême, in Bordeaux on 24 August 1200. A first child was born to John and Isabella in 1207, seven years after their marriage – so justifying the need for a governess but too long after the marriage for Isabella to have waited for the redemption of the boon, especially for so unlikely a purpose as the pardoning of three outlaws

Henry II, the father of both Richard and John, recovered Carlisle from the Scots in 1157 but at this stage he had already been married for five years and had been king for three years. It does not seem entirely credible that so determined a woman as Eleanor of Aquitaine would have waited so long to demand the redemption of a boon promised on her wedding unless for some substantial reason (although it may, perhaps, have been redeemable on his accession which makes it only three years). On the other hand she was reputedly promiscuous and she might have found the outlaws sexually attractive especially as she was eleven years older than her husband who was only 24 in 1157 – William of Cloudesley may have been more of her own age than her husband since he had a seven year old son. Eleanor had first been married at the age of about fifteen to the French king, Louis VII, and is subsequently said to have had a number of affairs including one with the nine-year-old Saladin while accompanying her husband on the disastrous second Crusade. The marriage to Louis was annulled in 1152 on the grounds of consanguinity and Eleanor seduced Henry and later married him on 18th May, barely two months later, when she was thirty years old and Henry only nineteen.

Henry and Eleanor had had four children by the summer following the king's recovery of Carlisle from the Scots. They were William (who had died in 1156), Henry (born 1155), Matilda (born 1156) and Richard (born 1157). A fifth (Geoffrey) was to be born 23 September 1158. Undoubtedly, Eleanor would have had a nursery and the prospective birth in September might have concentrated her mind on the need for a nursery governess.

The faltering match between the ballad and the history of Henry II does not allow us confidently to assign the events so precisely described to any exact period in history.

OUTLAWS OF INGLEWOOD

But there *is* a faltering match and, even if the analysis is somewhat forced, it provides some justification for placing *Outlaws of Inglewood* in 1158, the year after Henry II recovered Carlisle from the Scots. Henry, although a Norman, was the first of the Angevin kings of England, so justifying the idea that, as a new overlord, he might be less jealous of the Norman or Scottish rights to a monopoly of hunting privileges. Also by that time, the fortifications of Carlisle had been completed some years before, time perhaps for some 'crevices' through which the swineherd could escape to have developed in the walls. By that time, too, Carlisle Priory (1122) had been founded. The possibility that the priory was an Arroassian foundation at the time is

POSTSCRIPT

ignored.

Whether Armathwaite Priory had been founded by 1158 is uncertain. A supposed charter of 1089 is stated by Knowles and Hadcock, noted authorities, to be spurious but it had been established by c.1200 and an earlier date is not precluded. The legend states quite clearly that it was William's intention to place Alys and the two boys in a nunnery and it had to be somewhere! Perhaps a better candidate exists but Armathwaite was well located and the story is, after all, legend.

Richard de Tilliol, who does not figure in the original legend, was granted the manor of Scaleby early in the 12th century but lost it under the Scottish hegemony. Henry restored it to Richard's grandson, Peter, when Carlisle reverted to England although no building is recorded until later. But the story makes no assumption of any buildings – so that's all right!

As has been noted, later tradition seems to place Adam Bell and his associates roughly contemporaneously with, or perhaps a little earlier than, Robin Hood. Placing the action of the story in 1158 is consistent with the (admittedly tenuous) links with Robin. In the modern stories (though not the old ballads) Robin swears allegiance to Richard I who came to the throne thirty-one years later in 1189. This chronology accords reasonably well with the idea that Robin's father engaged in an archery contest with the Inglewood outlaws and that Adam was an old man when he kidnapped the sheriff's nephew and Robin sided with the sheriff to rescue Much in the *Robin of Sherwood* television series.

It is inevitable that there will be errors or inconsistencies in combining a fictional ballad with real history to produce a story – and no claim is made that *Outlaws of Inglewood* is anything other than a story. Henry and Eleanor may or may not have been in London during the summer of 1158 and Henry, like other kings of the time, apparently did not speak English (although he is said to have understood it) so could not have conversed directly with Adam. Peter de Tilliol may never have visited Carlisle or London at that time and certainly there is no evidence, other than the very dubious evidence of the ballad itself, that Adam Bell, Clym of the Clough and William of Cloudesley ever existed. The name given to Nell in the story is made up and (apart from the evidence of *Young Cloudesley*) we have no clue as the name of William's son. It would be tedious to enumerate other guesses. Nevertheless, it is hoped that the attempt to merge history and ballad has been worthwhile and that it has served to bring this, often forgotten, tradition to the attention of a wider public.

No doubt, the analysis can be challenged. So be it. The legend is, after all, only a legend and there is insufficient internal evidence in the ballad for confidence. Nevertheless, *Outlaws of Inglewood*, has adopted these assumptions.

CONCLUSION

Some other points are worth a mention.

Firstly, there is a need for an admission. It must at once be acknowledged that the events described in the prologue to *Outlaws of Inglewood* are the present author's invention, they serve merely to provide a sensible context to the more important events that follow and which are almost entirely derived from the original legend, although some detail has been added. Those who are interested, are encouraged to read the original legend which is included in this book. It is hoped that the additions do not alter the story unreasonably.

Secondly, in John Byddel's version of the legend, the story ends with the former outlaws going to Rome to seek pardon whereas later versions (including Copland's) simply say 'to some bysshop wyl we wend' – a much less positive statement. It is, perhaps, noteworthy that the period between the printing of the Byddel version (1536) and the printing of the Copland version (c.1565) coincides more or less with major convulsions in religious practice following the renunciation by Henry VIII of papal supremacy and his proclamation appointing himself, through the Act of Supremacy of 1534, as head of the church in England. Bydell's version, as the earlier idea, has been adopted in *Outlaws of Inglewood*.

Thirdly, Child's (1861) version has the queen giving William a salary of seventeen pence a day whereas other versions (including the 1957 version of Child) give twelve pence – probably a more likely figure and, therefore, adopted in *Outlaws of Inglewood*.

Fourthly, the mention in the ballad of silk for the strings of the outlaws' bows is interesting. Silk would have been very expensive in the 12th century but J Walker McSpadden, in his story of Robin

POSTSCRIPT

Hood (unusually, like *Outlaws,* set in the reign of Henry II), refers to "stout bows of cunning make, with fine waxen silk strings" which were given to Robin Hood and his men by Sir Richard of the Lea (*sic*) in return for Robin's help (although the original ballad says merely that they were "well ydyght", that is, well made).

Roberts, writing in 1801, says that there is no record or tradition of anything other than hemp being used for English bows. He goes on, however, to cite the legend of Adam Bell, implying that this is the first reference to silk strings in England. He says that, if silk was used, it must have been of raw silk twisted (if the elastic quality of silk could have been diminished and if the fibres were long enough) because strings made of threads bound at intervals like those used in Turkish, Persian and Tartar bows would have been too thick for the nock of English arrows. This may suggest that this part of the legend at least is somewhat later than the events described.

Fifthly, an outstanding feature of the chronicle is the shooting of an apple from young Will's head and its parallel with the legend of William Tell. It should be said that the apple-on-the-head theme is not by any means restricted to the William Tell and Adam Bell traditions and can be found in many legends from Switzerland northwards to Scandinavia. Child (1957) gives an account of this aspect of the story but it is interesting to note that the first printed reference to William Tell's feat is apparently found in the *White Book of Sarnen* dated about 1470, almost forty years after the appearance of Adam Bell and his friends in the Wiltshire parliamentary return – although the latter does not mention the apple motif.

Finally, a word of acknowledgement and of warning. I am indebted to many authors whose work I have consulted. Their names are included in the bibliography. If I have misunderstood anything, it is my fault not theirs. Rigorous students should read their books and decide for themselves.

BIBLIOGRAPHICAL NOTES

A study of the legend of Adam Bell quickly demonstrates that the information in many of the publications derives more or less extensively from other, earlier works, notably that of Child. This is not, in itself, reprehensible – indeed much of the postscript to this book is derivative. Unfortunately, the citations in some otherwise excellent publications are often absent or inadequate so one is not able to check them.

Sometimes, the information in one publication conflicts with that in another and, often, the language of earlier works is obscure or assumes a level of scholarship which is not justifiable in an age when it cannot automatically be supposed that interested readers will have had a literary training. It is beyond the scope of this book to adjudicate between publications but the following notes recognise works I have found valuable – as well as some which I have seen cited but have not seen.

I have not generally relied on any one publication and have not, therefore, felt it necessary in what is, after all, a general publication to provide detailed citations. Interested readers are invited to explore.

Web addresses (URLs) were correct at the time of writing but they, and the contents, are liable to change.

ANDREW of Wyntoun – see Knight and Ohlgren (3).

ANONYMOUS, 1976, A typescript, with a handwritten addition, relating to the stained glass in The Yate Chapel window is in the Gloucestershire Archives as document P63MI8.

BARBER Richard, *The Devil's Crown, A History of Henry II and his Sons*, London, British Broadcasting Corporation, 1978.

CARBONELL Jose Manuel, *La Cenicienta*, Barcelona, Editorial Bruguera, 1963 (see Hahn p.240).

CHILD Francis James (Ed.), *English and Scottish Ballads, Volume V*, London, Sampson Low, 1861.

CHILD Francis James (Ed.) *The English and Scottish Popular Ballads, Part V, Volume III*, Boston and New York, Houghton and Miflin, 1888.

CHILD Francis James (Ed.), *The English and Scottish Popular Ballads in Five Volumes, Volume III,* New York, Folklore Press, 1957.

COLLIER, J Payne, *Old Popular Poetry: "Adam Bell, Clym of the Clough and William of Clowdesly*, in "Notes and Queries", Issue 184, 7 May 1853. See http://www.gutenberg.org/files/20407/20407-8.txt

DAVENANT Sir William – an extract text from 'The Long Vacation in London' is found in "The Archers' Guide", 1833, by an Old Toxophoplite. See http://www.archerylibrary.com/books/guide/docs/chapter2_3.html

DOBSON R B and TAYLOR J, *Rymes of Robyn Hood*, London, Heinemann, 1976.

DREW John H, *Kenilworth, an Historical Miscellany*, Kenilworth (?), Pleasaunce Press, 1969.

DUNBAR William – See LAING

EBBUTT Maud Isabel, *Hero-Myths and Legends of the British Race*, London, Harrap, 1910.
See http://www.sacred-texts.com/neu/eng/hml/hml15.htm

EGAN Pierce (The Younger), *Adam Bell, Clym o'the Cleugh, and William of Cloudeslie*, London, Hextall, 1842.

GILPIN Sidney, *The Songs and Ballads of Cumberland and the Lake Country*, London, John Russell Smith *and* Carlisle, G & T Coward, 1874.

HAHN Thomas, 'Adam Bell, Clim of the Clough and William of Cloudesley' in OHLGREN Thomas H (Ed.), *Medieval Outlaws, Ten Tales in Modern English*, Stroud, Sutton Publishing, 1998.

HARVEY Sir Paul (Ed.), *The Oxford Companion to English Literature*, Oxford, Clarendon Press, 1967 (1973 edition).

BIBLIOGRAPHICAL NOTES

HOLT J C, *Robin Hood*, London, Thames and Hudson, Revised 1989.

HOROWITZ Anthony, *Robin Hood and the Outlaw Adam Bell*, from HTV/Goldcrest 'Robin of Sherwood' television series and first broadcast in 1986. Some information can be found by searching the web but the site used for this book is no longer available.

HUNT Roderick, *Myths and Legends*, Oxford Junior Readers 5, Oxford, OUP, 1981. (Not seen, but see Hahn, p.240.)

HUNTER Joseph, *New Illustrations of the Life, Studies, and Writings of Shakespeare*, London, 1845. (Not seen but see Child (1861), pp.126-127 and Dobson and Taylor, p.260 note 2.)

IMAGES OF CUMBRIA (extracts from Mannix and Whelan, *History, Gazetteer and Directory of Cumberland,* 1847). http://www.stevebulman.f9.co.uk/cumbria/frames_home.html Select "parish index".

JONSON Ben, *The Alchemist*, text at www.levity.com/alchemy/jn-alch1.html.

KEEN Maurice, *The Outlaws of Medieval Legend*, (3rd edition, Routledge and Kegan Paul, 1961. (Not seen)

KINSLEY James (Ed.), *The Oxford Book of Ballads*, Oxford at the Clarendon Press, 1969.

KNIGHT Stephen and OHLGREN Thomas H [1], *Adam Bell, Clym of the Clough and William of Cloudesley*, Originally published in 'Robin Hood and Other Outlaw Tales', Kalamazoo, Michigan, Medieval Institute Publications, 1997 and republished at www.lib.rochester.edu/camelot/teams/adamint.htm

KNIGHT Stephen and OHLGREN Thomas H [2], *Robin Hood's Birth, Breeding, Valour, and Marriage*, Originally published in 'Robin Hood and Other Outlaw Tales', Kalamazoo, Michigan, Medieval Institute Publications, 1997 and republished at www.lib.rochester.edu/camelot/teams/birthint.htm

KNIGHT Stephen and OHLGREN Thomas H [3], *Andrew of Wyntoun's Oryginale Chronicle* originally published in 'Robin Hood and Other Outlaw Tales', Kalamazoo, Michigan, Medieval Institute Publications, 1997 and republished at www.lib.rochester.edu/camelot/teams/orygnale.htm

BIBLIOGRAPHICAL NOTES

KNOWLES David and HADCOCK R Neville, *Medieval Religious Houses – England and Wales*, London, Longman, 1971.

LAING David (Ed.) *The Poems of William Dunbar*, Volume 1, Edinburgh, Laing and Forbes *and* London, William Pickering, 1834.

LANSING Marion Florence, *Life in the Greenwood – Robin Hood Tales*, Boston, Athenaum Press, Ginn, 1909. (Not seen.)

MARSHALL Hilda (?), *Who do you think you are, Adam Bell?,* in 'Cousins 8' at www.etext.org/Zines/ASCII/ Then select Cousins, then cous8pt2 and then search on Adam Bell.

McSPADDEN J Walker, *Robin Hood*, Originally published in 1904 but now available in new editions (which have not been seen). See http://www.worldwideschool.org/library/books/lit/adventure/RobinHood/chap21.html

PHILLIPS Graham and KEATMAN Martin, *Robin Hood – The Man Behind the Myth*, London, Michael O'Mara Books, 1995.

PUTTENHAM George (attrib.), *The Arte of English Poesie: Book II*, London, Richard Field, 1589. Text at http://rpo.library.utoronto.ca/display/displayprose.cfm?prosenum=17&subfile=puttenham_artofp_all.html

PYLE Howard, *The Merry Adventures of Robin Hood*, New York, Charles Scribner's Sons, 1883. Text at http://www.classicreader.com/read.php/sid.1/bookid.277/sec.1/

RITSON Joseph, *Pieces of Ancient Popular Poetry*, 1791 (Not seen but see Child, 1957 p.15).

ROBERSON Jennifer, *Lady of the Forest*, New York, Kensington, 1992.

ROBERT TEMPLE BOOKSELLERS, (biographical note on Pierce Egan). http://www.polybiblio.com/templar/QCRT801159.html

ROBERTS T, *The English Bowman*, London, Author, 1801. Text at www.archerylibrary.com/books/english_bowman/html/123.htm

SARGENT Helen Child and KITTERIDGE George Lyman (Eds), *English and Scottish Popular Ballads, edited from the collection of Francis James Child*, London, David Nutt, 1905 *and* Boston and New York, Houghton Mifflin.

BIBLIOGRAPHICAL NOTES

WESTWOOD Jennifer, *Tales and Legends*, Granada Publishing but first published in London by Hart-Davis, 1971.

WILLIAMSON David, *Kings and Queens of Britain*, originally published by Webb and Bower and republished in Leicester by the Promotional Reprint Company for Bookmart, 1991.

WORDSWORTH William, sonnet *Suggested by a View from an Eminence in Inglewood Forest* in 'The Poetical Works of Wordsworth', London, Frederick Warne, undated.

THE ORIGINAL BALLAD OF
Adam Bel, Clym of the Cloughe, and Wyllyam of Cloudeslè

adapted from *English and Scottish Ballads*, volume V,
edited by Francis James Child
Sampson Low, Son, & Co., 47 Ludgate Hill, London, 1861
(Printed from Ritson's edition of Copland's text 'with some important improvements derived from a transcript of Mr. Collier's[*] fragment most kindly furnished by that gentleman')
Child's parenthetic insertions have been silently assimilated.

THE FIRST FITT

Mery it was in grene forest,
Amonge the leues grene,
Wher that men walke east and west,
With bowes and arrowes kene,

To ryse the dere out of theyr denne,—
Such sightes hath ofte bene sene,—
As by thre yemen of the north countrey,
By them it is I meane.

The one of them hight Adam Bel,
The other Clym of the Clough,
The thyrd was William of Cloudesly,
An archer good ynough.

They were outlawed for venyson,
These yemen everechone;
They swore them brethren upon a day,
To Englysshe-wood for to gone.

Now lith and lysten, gentylmen,
That of myrthes loveth to hear:
Two of them were single men,
The third had a wedded fere.

Wyllyam was the wedded man,
Muche more then was hys care:
He sayde to hys brethren upon a day,
To Carelel he would fare,

For to speke with fayre Alse hys wife,
And with hys chyldren thre.
"By my trouth," sayde Adam Bel,
"Not by the counsell of me.

"For if ye go to Caerlel, brother,
And from thys wylde wode wende,
If the justice mai you take,
Your lyfe were at an ende."

"If that I come not tomorowe, brother,
By pryme to you agayne,
Truste not els but that I am take,
Or else that I am slayne."

He toke hys leave of his brethren two,
And to Carlel he is gon;
There he knocked at hys owne windowe,
Shortlye and anone.

"Where be you, fayre Alyce, my wyfe,
And my chyldren three?
Lyghtly let in thyne owne husbande,
Wyllyam of Cloudeslè."

"Alas!" then sayde fayre Alyce,
And syghed wonderous sore,
"Thys place hath ben besette for you,
Thys half yere and more."

"Now am I here," sayde Cloudeslè,
"I woulde that I in were:—
Now feche us meate and drynke ynoughe,
And let us make good chere."

She fetched him meat and drynke plenty,
Lyke a true wedded wyfe,
And pleased hym wyth that she had,
Whome she loved as her lyfe.

There lay an old wyfe in that place,
A lytle besyde the fyre,
Whych Wyllyam had found, of cherytye,
More then seven yere.

Up she rose and walked full styll,
Evel mote she spede therefoore,
For she had not set no fote on ground
In seven yere before

---

[*] Presumably J Payne Collier – see Bibliography.

THE ORIGINAL BALLAD

She went unto the justice hall,
As fast as she could hye;
"Thys nyght is come unto this town
Wyllyam of Cloudeslè."

Thereof the iustice was full fayne,
And so was the shirife also;
"Thou shalt not travaile hether, dame, for nought,
Thy meed thou shalt have or thou go."

They gave to her a ryght good goune,
Of scarlat it was, as I heard sayne;
She toke the gyft and home she wente,
And couched her downe agayne.

They rysed the towne of mery Carlel,
In all the hast that they can,
And came thronging to Wyllyames house,
As fast as they myght gone.

Theyr they besette that good yeman,
Round about on every syde,
Wyllyam hearde great noyse of folkes,
That heytherward they hyed.

Alyce opened a shot-wyndow,
And loked all about,
She was ware of the justice and shirife bothe,
Wyth a full great route.

"Alas! treason," cry'd Aleyce,
"Ever wo may thou be!
Go into my chambre, my husband," she sayd,
"Swete Wyllyam of Cloudeslè."

He toke hys sweard and hys bucler,
Hys bow and hys chyldren thre,
And wente into hys strongest chamber,
Where he thought surest to be.

Fayre Alice folowed him as a lover true,
With a pollaxe in her hande;
"He shal be dead that here cometh in
Thys dore, whyle I may stand."

Cloudeslè bent a wel good bowe,
That was of trusty tre,
He smot the justise on the brest,
That hys arrowe brest in thre.

"God's curse on his hartt," saide William,
"Thys day thy cote dyd on;
If it had ben no better then myne,
It had gone nere thy bone."

"Yelde the, Cloudeslè," sayd the justise,
"And thy bowe and thy arrowes the fro:"
"Gods curse on hys hart," sayde fair Alice,
"That my husband councelleth so."

"Set fyre on the house," saide the sherife,
"Syth it wyll no better be,
And brenne we therin William," he saide,
"Hys wyfe and chyldren thre."

They fyred the house in many a place,
The fyre flew upon hye;
"Alas!" then cryed fayr Alice,
"I se we here shall dy."

William openyd hys backe wyndow,
That was in hys chambre on hye,
And wyth shetes let hys wyfe downe,
And hys chyldren thre.

"Have here my treasure," sayde William,
"My wyfe and my chyldren thre,
For Christes love do them no harme,
But wreke you all on me."

Wyllyam shot so wonderous well,
Tyll hys arrowes were all ygo,
And the fyre so fast upon hym fell,
That hys bowstryng brent in two.

The spercles brent and fell hym on,
Good Wyllyam of Cloudeslè!
But than wax he a wofull man,
And sayde, "thys is a cowardes death to me.

"Leuer I had," sayde Wyllyam,
"With my sworde in the route to renne,
Then here among myne ennemyes wode,
Thus cruelly to bren."

He toke hys sweard and hys bucklier,
And among them all he ran;
Where the people were most in prece,
He smot downe many a man.

There myght no man stand hys stroke,
So fersly on them he ran;
Then they threw wyndowes and dores on him,
And so toke that good yemàn.

There they hym bounde both hande and fote,
And in depe dongeon hym cast;
"Now, Cloudeslè," sayd the hye justice,
"Thou shalt be hanged in hast."

THE ORIGINAL BALLAD

"One vow shal I make," sayd the sherife,
"A payre of newe galowes shall I for the make,
And the gates of Caerlel shal be shutte,
There shall no man come in therat.

"Then shall not helpe Clim of the Cloughe,
Nor yet shall Adam Bell,
Though they came with a thousand mo,
Nor all the devels in hell."

Early in the mornyng the justice uprose,
To the gates first gan he gon,
And commaundede to be shut full cloce
Lightilè everychone.

Then went he to the market place,
As fast as he coulde hye;
A payre of new gallous there did he up set,
Besyde the pyllory.

A lytle boy stod them amonge,
And asked what meaned that gallow tre;
They sayde, "to hange a good yeamàn,
Called Wyllyam of Cloudeslè."

That lytle boye was the towne swyne-heard,
And kept fayre Alyce swyne,
Oft he had seene Cloudeslè in the wodde,
And geuen hym there to dyne.

He went out att a creves in the wall,
And lightly to the wood dyd gone;
There met he with these wight yonge men,
Shortly and anone.

"Alas!" then sayde that lytle boye,
"Ye tary here all to longe;
Cloudeslè is taken and dampned to death,
All readye for to honge."

"Alas!" than sayde good Adam Bell,
"That ever we see thys daye!
He myght her with us have dwelled,
So ofte as we dyd him praye!

"He myght have taryed in grene foreste,
Under the shadowes sheene,
And have kepte both hym and us in reaste,
Out of trouble and teene!"

Adam bent a ryght good bow,
A great hart sone had he slayne;
"Take that, chylde," he sayde, "to thy dynner,
And bryng me myne arrowe agayne."

"Now go we hence," sayed these wight yong men,
"Tary we no lenger here;
We shall hym borowe, by gods grace,
Though we bye it full dere."

To Caerlel went these good yemèn,
On a mery mornyng of Maye:
Here is a fyt of Cloudesli,
And another is for to saye.

THE SECOND FITT

And when they came to mery Caerlell,
In a fayre mornyng tyde,
They founde the gates shut them untyll,
Round about on every syde.

"Alas!" than sayd good Adam Bell,
"That ever we were made men!
These gates be shut so wonderly wel,
That we may not come here in."

Then spake him Clym of the Clough,
"Wyth a wyle we wyl us in bryng;
Let us saye we be messengers,
Streyght comen from our king."

Adam said, "I have a letter written wel,
Now let us wysely werke;
We wyl saye we have the kinges scale,
I holde the porter no clerke."

Then Adam Bell bete on the gate,
With strokes great and strong;
The porter herde suche noyse therat,
And to the gate faste he throng.

"Who is there nowe," sayde the porter,
"That maketh all thys knocking?
"We be tow messengers," sayde Clim of the Clough,
"Be comen streyght from our kyng."

"We haue a letter," sayd Adam Bel,
"To the justice we must it bryng;
Let us in, our messag to do,
That we were agayne to our kyng."

"Here commeth no man in," sayd the porter,
"By hym that dyed on a tre,
Tyll a false thefe be hanged,
Called Wyllyam of Cloudeslè."

THE ORIGINAL BALLAD

Then spake the good yeman Clym of the Clough,
And swore by Mary fre,
"And if that we stande longe wythout,
Lyke a thefe hanged shalt thou be.

"Lo here we have the kynges seale;
What! lordeyne, art thou wode?"
The porter went it had ben so,
And lyghtly dyd of hys hode.

"Welcome be my lordes seale," he saide,
"For that ye shall come in:"
He opened the gate full shortlye,
An evyl openyng for him.

"Now we are in," sayde Adam Bell,
"Thereof we are full faine,
But Christ knoweth that harowed hell,
How we shall com out agayne."

"Had we the keys," said Clim of the Clough,
"Ryght wel then shoulde we spede;
Then might we come out wel ynough,
When we se tyme and nede."

They called the porter to a counsell,
And wrange hys necke in two,
And caste him in a depe dongeòn,
And toke hys keys hym fro.

"Now am I porter," sayde Adam Bel,
"Se, brother, the keys haue we here;
The worst porter to merry Caerlel,
That ye had thys hundred yere.

"And now wyll we our bowes bend,
Into the towne wyll we go,
For to delyver our dere brother,
That lyveth in care and wo."

And thereupon they bent theyr bowes,
And loked theyr stringes were round;
The market place of mery Caerlel,
They beset in that stound.

And as they loked them besyde,
A paire of new galowes ther thei see,
And the justice with a quest of swerers,
That had judged Cloudeslè there hanged to be.

And Cloudeslè hymselfe lay redy in a carte,
Faste bounde both fote and hand,
And a stronge rop about hys necke,
All readye for to be hangde.

The justice called to him a ladde,
Cloudeslès clothes should he have,
To take the measure of that good yeman,
And therafter to make hys grave.

"I have seen as great a mearveile," said Cloudesli,
"As betwyene thys and pryme,
He that maketh thys grave for me,
Himselfe may lye therin."

"Thou speakest proudli," saide the justice,
"I shall the hange with my hande:"
Full wel that herd hys brethren two,
There styll as they dyd stande.

Then Cloudeslè cast hys eyen asyde,
And saw hys to brethren stande,
At a corner of the market place,
With theyr good bows bent in ther hand.

"I se good comfort," sayd Cloudeslè,
"Yet hope I well to fare;
If I might haue my handes at wyll,
Ryght lytle wolde I care."

Then spake good Adam Bell,
To Clym of the Clough so free,
"Brother, se ye marke the justyce wel,
Lo yonder ye may him see.

"And at the shyrife shote I wyll,
Strongly with an arrowe kene;
A better shote in mery Caerlel
Thys seven yere was not sene."

They lowsed their arrowes both at once,
Of no man had they dread;
The one hyt the justice, the other the sheryfe,
That both theyr sides gan blede.

All men voyded, that them stode nye,
When the justice fell downe to the grounde,
And the sherife fell nyghe hym by,
Eyther had his deathes wounde.

All the citezens fast gan flye,
They durst no longer abyde;
Then lyghtly they loused Cloudeslè,
When he with ropes lay tyde.

Wyllyam sterte to an officer of the towne,
Hys axe out of hys hande he wronge,
On eche syde he smote them downe,
Hym thought he taryed all to long.

Wyllyam sayde to hys brethren two,
"Thys daye let us togyder lyve and dye;
If ever you have nede as I have now,
The same shall you fynde by me."

They shot so well in that tyde,
For theyr stringes were of silke full sure,
That they kept the stretes on every side:
That batayle dyd longe endure.

They fought together as brethren tru,
Lyke hardy men and bolde;
Many a man to the ground they thrue,
And many a herte made colde.

But when their arrowes were all gon,
Men preced on them full fast;
They drew theyr swordes then anone,
And theyr bowes from them cast.

They went lyghtlye on theyr way,
Wyth swordes and buclers round;
By that it was the myddes of the day,
They had made mani a wound.

There was many an out-horne in Caerlel blowen,
And the belles bacward did they ryng;
Many a woman sayd alas,
And many theyr handes dyd wryng.

The mayre of Caerlel forth com was,
And with hym a ful great route;
These thre yemen dred him full sore,
For of theyr lyues they stode in great doute.

The mayre came armed a full great pace,
With a pollaxe in hys hande;
Many a strong man with him was,
There in that stowre to stande.

The mayre smot at Cloudeslè with his bil,
Hys bucler he brust in two;
Full many a yeman with great yll,
"Alas, treason!" they cryed for wo.
"Kepe we the gates fast," they bad,
"That these traytours thereout not go."

But al for nought was that they wrought,
For so fast they downe were layde,
Tyll they all thre, that so manfulli fought,
Were gotten without at a braide.

"Have here your keys," sayd Adam Bel,
"Myne office I here forsake;
Yf you do by my councèll,
A new porter do ye make."

He threw the keys there at theyr heads,
And bad them evell to thryve,
And all that letteth any good yeman
To come and comfort hys wyfe.

Thus be these good yemen gon to the wod,
As lyght as lefe on lynde;
They lough and be mery in theyr mode,
Theyr ennemyes were ferre behynd.

When they came to Englyshe wode,
Under the trysty tre,
There they found bowes full good,
And arrowes full great plentye.

"So God me help," sayd Adam Bell,
And Clym of the Clough so fre,
"I would we were nowe in mery Caerlel,
Before that fayre meyny."

They set them downe and made good chere,
And eate and drank full well:
Here is a fet of these wyght yong men,
And another I shall you tell.

THE THIRD FITT

As they sat in Englyshe-wood,
Under theyr trysty tre,
Them thought they herd a woman wepe,
But her they mought not se.

Sore then syghed the fayre Alyce,
And sayde, "Alas that ever I sawe this daye!
For now is my dere husband slayne,
Alas and wel a way!

"Myght I have spoken wyth hys dere brethren,
Or with eyther of them twayne,
To let them know what him befell
My hart were out of payne!"

Cloudeslè walked a lytle besyde,
And loked under the grenewood linde;
He was ware of hys wife and chyldren thre,
Full wo in hart and mynde.

THE ORIGINAL BALLAD

"Welcome, wife," then sayde Wyllyam,
"Under this trysty tre;
I had wende yesterday, by swete saynt John,
Thou shulde me never have se."

"Now well is me," she sayde, "that ye be here,
My hart is out of wo:"
"Dame," he sayde, "be mery and glad,
And thank my brethren two."

"Hereof to speake," sayd Adam Bell,
"I-wis it is no bote;
The meat that we must supp withall
It runneth yet fast on fote."

Then went they down into a launde,
These noble archares all thre,
Eche of them slew a hart of greece,
The best they could there se.

"Have here the best, Alyce my wife,"
Sayde Wyllyam of Cloudeslè,
"By cause ye so bouldly stod by me,
When I was slayne full nye."

Then went they to supper,
Wyth suche meat as they had,
And thanked God of ther fortune;
They were both mery and glad.

And when they had supped well,
Certayne without any leace,
Cloudeslè sayd, "We wyll to our kyng,
To get us a charter of peace.

"Alyce shall be at sojournyng,
In a nunry here besyde;
My tow sonnes shall wyth her go,
And ther they shall abyde.

"Myne eldest son shall go wyth me,
For hym have I no care,
And he shall breng you worde agayn
How that we do fare."

Thus be these yemen to London gone,
As fast as they might hye,
Tyll they came to the kynges pallace,
Where they woulde nedes be.

And whan they came to the kynges courte,
Unto the pallace gate,
Of no man wold they aske no leave,
But boldly went in therat.

They preced prestly into the hall,
Of no man had they dreade;
The porter came after and dyd them call,
And with them began to chyde.

The ussher sayed, "Yemen, what wold ye haue?
I pray you tell me;
You myght thus make offycers shent:
Good syrs, of whence be ye?"

"Syr, we be outlawes of the forest,
Certayne without any leace,
And hether we be come to our kyng,
To get us a charter of peace."

And whan they came before the kyng,
As it was the lawe of the lande,
They kneled downe without lettyng,
And eche held up his hand.

They sayed, "Lord, we beseche the here,
That ye wyll graunt us grace,
For we haue slaine your fat falow der,
In many a sondry place."

"What be your names?" then said our king,
"Anone that you tell me:
They sayd, "Adam Bel, Clim of the Clough,
And Wyllyam of Cloudeslè."

"Be ye those theves," then sayd our kyng,
"That men have tolde of to me?
Here to god I make a vowe,
Ye shal be hanged al thre.

"Ye shal be dead without mercy,
As I am kynge of this lande."
He commanded his officers everichone
Fast on them to lay hand.

There they toke these good yemen,
And arested them all thre:
"So may I thryve," sayd Adam Bell,
"Thys game lyketh not me.

"But, good lorde, we beseche you now,
That you graunt vs grace,
Insomuche as we be to you comen,
Or els that we may fro you passe,

"With such weapons as we have here,
Tyll we be out of your place;
And yf we lyve this hundreth yere,
We wyll aske you no grace."

THE ORIGINAL BALLAD

"Ye speake proudly," sayd the kynge,
"Ye shall be hanged all thre:"
"That were great pitye," then sayd the quene,
"If any grace myght be.

"My lorde, whan I came fyrst into this lande,
To be your wedded wyfe,
The fyrst bowne that I wold aske,
Ye would graunt it me belyfe;

"And I asked never none tyll now,
Therefore, good lorde, graunte it me."
"Now aske it, madam," sayd the kynge,
"And graunted shall it be."

"Then, my good lord, I you beseche,
These yemen graunt ye me:"
"Madame, ye myght have asked a bowne
That shuld have ben worth them all thre.

"Ye myght have asked towres and townes,
Parkes and forestes plenty."
"None so pleasaunt to mi pay," she said,
"Nor none so lefe to me."

"Madame, sith it is your desyre,
Your askyng graunted shal be;
But I had lever have geven you
Good market townes thre."

The quene was a glad woman,
And sayd, "Lord, gramarcy;
I dare undertake for them,
That true men shal they be.

"But, good lord, speke som mery word,
That comfort they may se."
"I graunt you grace," then said our king,
"Wasshe, felos, and to meate go ye."

They had not setten but a whyle,
Certayne without lesynge,
There came messengers out of the north,
With letters to our kynge.

And whan they came before the kynge,
They kneled downe vpon theyr kne,
And sayd, "Lord, your offycers grete you wel,
Of Caerlel in the north cuntrè."

"How fares my justice," sayd the kyng,
"And my sherife also?"
"Syr, they be slayne, without leasynge,
And many an officer mo."

"Who hath them slayne?" sayd the kyng,
"Anone thou tell me:"
"Adam Bel, and Clime of the Clough,
And Wyllyam of Cloudeslè."

"Alas for rewth!" then sayd our kynge,
"My hart is wonderous sore;
I had leuer than a thousand pounde,
I had knowne of thys before.

"For I have graunted them grace,
And that forthynketh me,
But had I knowne all thys before,
They had been hanged all thre."

The kyng opened the letter anone,
Hymselfe he red it thro,
And founde how these thre outlawes had slaine
Thre hundred men and mo.

Fyrst the justice and the sheryfe,
And the mayre of Caerlel towne;
Of all the constables and catchipolles
Alyve were left not one.

The baylyes and the bedyls both,
And the sergeauntes of the law,
And forty fosters of the fe,
These outlawes had yslaw,

And broke his parks, and slaine his dere;
Over all they chose the best;
So perelous outlawes as they were,
Walked not by easte nor west.

When the kynge this letter had red,
In hys harte he syghed sore;
"Take vp the table anone," he bad,
"For I may eate no more."

The kyng called hys best archars,
To the buttes with hym to go;
"I wylle se these felowes shote," he sayd,
In the north have wrought this wo."

The kynges bowmen buske them blyve,
And the quenes archers also,
So dyd these thre wyght yemèn,
Wyth them they thought to go.

There twyse or thryse they shote about,
For to assay theyr hande;
There was no shote these yemen shot,
That any prycke myght them stand.

THE ORIGINAL BALLAD

Then spake Wyllyam of Cloudeslè,
"By him that for me dyed,
I hold hym never no good archar
That shuteth at buttes so wyde."

"Wherat?" then sayd our kyng.
"I pray thee tell me:"
"At such a but, syr," he sayd,
"As men use in my countree."

Wyllyam went into a fyeld,
And his to brethren with him,
There they set vp to hasell roddes,
Twenty score paces betwene.

"I hold him an archar," said Cloudeslè,
"That yonder wande cleveth in two:"
"Here is none suche," sayd the kyng,
"Nor none that can so do."

"I shall assaye, syr," sayd Cloudeslè,
"Or that I farther go:"
Cloudeslè, with a bearyng arow,
Clave the wand in to.

"Thou art the best archer," then said the king,
"Forsothe that ever I se:"
"And yet for your love," said Wylliam,
"I wyll do more maystry.

"I have a sonne is seven yere olde,
He is to me full deare;
I wyll hym tye to a stake,
All shall se that be here;

"And lay an apele upon hys head,
And go syxe score paces hym fro,
And I myselfe, with a brode arow,
Shall cleve the apple in two."

"Now haste the," then sayd the kyng,
"By him that dyed on a tre;
But yf thou do not as thou hast sayde,
Hanged shalt thou be.

"And thou touche his head or gowne,
In syght that men may se,
By all the sayntes that be in heaven,
I shall hange you all thre."

"That I have promised," said William,
"I wyl it never forsake;"
And there even before the kynge,
In the earth he droue a stake,

And bound therto his eldest sonne,
And bad hym stande styll therat,
And turned the childes face fro him,
Because he shuld not sterte.

An apple upon his head he set,
And then his bowe he bent;
Syxe score paces they were out met,
And thether Cloudeslè went.

There he drew out a fayr brode arrowe,
Hys bowe was great and longe,
He set that arrowe in his bowe,
That was both styffe and stronge.

He prayed the people that was there,
That they would styll stande,
"For he that shooteth for such a wager,
Behoveth a stedfast hand."

Muche people prayed for Cloudeslè,
That hys lyfe saved myght be,
And whan he made hym redy to shote,
There was many a weping eye.

Thus Cloudeslè clefte the apple in two,
That many a man myght se;
"Over gods forbode," sayde the kynge,
"That thou shote at me!

"I geve the xviii. pence a day,
And my bowe shalt thou beare,
And over all the north countre,
I make the chyfe rydere."

"And I geve the xvii. pence a day," said the quene,
"By god and by my fay;
Come feche thy payment when thou wylt,
No man shall say the nay.

"Wyllyam, I make the a gentelman,
Of clothyng and of fe,
And thi two brethren yemen of my chambre,
For they are so semely to se.

"Your sonne, for he is tendre of age,
Of my wyne-seller shall he be,
And whan he commeth to mannes estate,
Better avaunced shall he be.

"And, Wylliam, bring me your wife," said the quene,
"Me longeth her sore to se;
She shal be my chefe gentelwoman,
To governe my nursery."

THE ORIGINAL BALLAD

The yemen thanketh them full curteously,
And sayde, "To some bysshop wyl we wend,
 Of all the synnes that we have done
 To be assoyld at his hand."

So forth be gone these good yemen,
 As fast as they myght hye,
And after came and dwelled with the kynge,
 And dyed good men all thre.

Thus endeth the lives of these good yemen,
 God send them eternall blysse,
And all that with hande bowe shoteth,
 That of heaven may never mysse!
